The Literacy Kit

Inform, Explain, Describe

Teacher's Book

Geoff Barton   Michaela Blackledge

Joanna Crewe   Jane Flintoft   Becca Heddle

OXFORD

OXFORD
UNIVERSITY PRESS

Great Clarendon Street, Oxford OX2 6DP

Oxford University Press is a department of the University of Oxford.
It furthers the University's objective of excellence in research, scholarship,
and education by publishing worldwide in

Oxford New York

Auckland Bangkok Buenos Aires Cape Town Chennai
Dar es Salaam Delhi Hong Kong Istanbul Karachi Kolkata
Kuala Lumpur Madrid Melbourne Mexico City Mumbai Nairobi
São Paulo Shanghai Taipei Tokyo Toronto

Oxford is a registered trade mark of Oxford University Press
in the UK and in certain other countries

British Library Cataloguing in Publication Data

Data available

ISBN 0 19 832041 8

3 5 7 9 10 8 6 4

Designed and set by Zed, Oxford

Printed in Great Britain by Alden Press Ltd, Oxford

CONTENTS

Photocopy masters

Unit 1 PCM A Healthy eating

Unit 2 PCM A My first day at school

Unit 2 PCM B My first day at school

Unit 3 PCM A Similarities and differences

Unit 5 PCM A Planning a description

Unit 6 PCM A Writing a formal newspaper report: 1

Unit 6 PCM B Writing a formal newspaper report: 2

Unit 7 PCM A Autobiographical writing

Unit 8 PCM A Florence Nightingale

Unit 9 PCM A Writing survey: writing for different subjects

Unit 9 PCM B Writing an explanation

Unit 10 PCM A Writing an informal newspaper report

Unit 11 PCM A Describing a journey

Unit 12 PCM A Writing a leaflet

Unit 13 PCM A Tollund Man History assignment

Unit 13 PCM B Tollund Man English assignment

Unit 14 PCM A Writing a parody: estate agent's report

General PCM 1 Brainstorming

General PCM 2 Brainstorming for arguments

General PCM 3 Key words

General PCM 4 Research grid

General PCM 5 Information

General PCM 6 Recount

General PCM 7 Explanation

General PCM 8 Types of writing used in subjects

General PCM 9 Conventions of different types of writing

General PCM 10 Instruction texts

General PCM 11 Speaking and listening

INTRODUCTION

The National Strategy English Strand

Welcome to *The Literacy Kit*. This teacher's book will provide advice on and resources for implementing the National Strategy at Key Stage 3 into your scheme of work using *The Literacy Kit*.

Literacy lessons

In order to improve continuity of teaching and learning from Key Stage 2 to 3, NLS advocates the following interactive lesson structure.

1. A short lesson starter activity.
2. An introduction to the main learning objectives for the lesson.
3. Development of the main learning objectives.
4. A plenary session, consolidating the learning and pointing the way to the next step.

This structure is designed to break the lesson into more manageable 'chunks' for students to help sustain their levels of concentration.

Ten-minute lesson starters

Starter activities should:

♦ last approximately ten minutes
♦ be fast, focused and highly interactive in style
♦ focus attention
♦ involve everyone, and create communal learning.
♦ be ideal for spelling, vocabulary and some sentence level work
♦ allow for assessment and intervention in misunderstanding.

Students often need something to refocus their attention at the start of a lesson – immediately – and interest them in the learning so that they want to question, to investigate, to become independent learners. The fast pace of the session doesn't cater for distraction or boredom!

The active nature of each starter task appeals to all abilities of students. We all learn in different ways and, with a combination of oral, writing and active starters, you create a more productive learning atmosphere. The enthusiasm created lifts the confidence of all students to 'have a go' and not be afraid of failure. From the teacher's point of view, it allows immediate assessment, and intervention in misunderstanding and mistakes, which in turn provides positive opportunities for support and extension.

Planning starters into literacy lessons

When including starter activities in your schemes of work, bear in mind that they do not always have to directly link to the main teaching objectives of the lesson. However, many schools have identified that starter activities can also successfully link to the full lesson. Starter activities are a great tool for 'assessment for learning'. Identified student weaknesses can be addressed through starter activities, which can easily be incorporated into short-term planning.

For further advice and resourcing of starter activities, consult *The Literacy Kit Word Level* and *Sentence Level Lesson Starters* activity boxes, described on page 7.

Whole class teaching

Within the introduction of the lessons, teachers need to headline the learning objectives. This whole class session can provide the opportunity to look at aspects of the teaching sequences, through modelling and shared work. This communal approach focuses all students and provides a structure for the learning.

Modelled reading and writing

Teacher modelling provides students with a model of how to apply an objective in independent work. The teacher, as expert, explicitly demonstrates the cognitive processes and skills an independent learner goes through. They show how to write/read/think/talk/listen according to the specifications of the objective. This process offers support to students, enabling them to access and use the objective confidently.

Shared reading and writing

Shared reading and writing provide an opportunity for students to tackle texts and concepts which would normally be out of reach. Shared work allows for whole class learning. The teacher direction, along with peer support, offers a stepping stone towards independent reading and writing. In shared writing, the teacher acting as scribe allows students to be free from the difficulties of writing, and participate in planning, composing, redrafting, editing and publishing texts.

Development

The development session allows students to apply what they have learned in the initial stages of the lesson. This may be independently or in smaller groups. However, the structure of the lesson can be flexible, allowing for a longer session. This can provide an opportunity to complete extended pieces of work.

Guided reading and writing

Guided reading and writing can be an opportunity to support a small group while the majority of the class work independently on the development activity. Guided sessions enable teachers to intervene at the point of the students applying their learning in order to have immediate impact. A community of readers and writers can be established where peers feel comfortable sharing, discussing and analysing each other's work, developing and supporting their application and understanding of the objective.

Plenaries

The plenary session should consolidate the learning objectives of the lesson with the whole class. It can clarify misconceptions, and should point the way to the next stage. This is an invaluable point for teachers to assess student understanding, and identify any need for revisiting the objective.

Your questions answered

Q How much extra work is involved – will I have to abandon my existing schemes of work.

A Don't automatically throw out your existing scheme of work! Look at it alongside the *Framework* – what works, what can be adapted, and what needs replacing? It will take time when you initially audit your schemes of work, and identify gaps. *The Literacy Kit* is designed to allow you to dip in and out, to fill these gaps when they arise. *The Literacy Kit* can also be used more comprehensively, as all activities are directly linked to the *Framework* objectives.

Q I've heard that we should be 'clustering' word, sentence and text level objectives. How do we go about this?

A The *Framework* has logical links across the objectives in word, sentence and text level columns. *The Literacy Kit* addresses these logical links within the units of work, and clearly states which objectives have been employed. The teaching notes in this *Teacher's Book* give comprehensive information on the objectives taught in each unit of the students' book. The 'dip-in' nature of *The Literacy Kit* allows you to remain creative with your own schemes of work.

Q We have a large department. Do we all have to teach the same thing at the same time?

A Although smaller departments may find fully collaborative planning useful, larger departments of course need to share resources effectively. To avoid repeating work, departments can build in to their central bank of resources a bank of short and medium plans which each creatively adhere to the department's schemes of work. The 'dip in' nature of *The Literacy Kit* resources enables teachers to use the activities effectively within individual or department plans.

Q Does the Kit dictate particular student groupings?

A The *Framework* is designed so that it can be taught to students in mixed ability classes or setted groups. The activities and resources within the Kit are linked directly to Framework objectives. A range of differentiated materials provide opportunities for teachers to plan lessons which will meet the needs of all student abilities, thereby supporting the literacy methodology.

Q How do I approach starter activities?

A Bear in mind that a successful starter activity is active, and involves everyone. All students should be effectively challenged, and focused on the objective. A range of activities should be employed, such as investigation, show-me and washing lines, which accommodate the different ways students learn. If you feel you could use assistance in the invention and production of starter activities, consult *The Literacy Kit Word Level* and *Sentence Level Lesson Starters* activity boxes. These have been created and tested by teachers and consultants from pilot authorities.

Q When in my literacy lessons should I use the students' books?

A You could use them for whole class teaching, sharing the text and discussing the questions before completing the writing activities during modelled writing. The books are also ideal for students to use independently. The structure replicates the model of reading a text, analysing its features, and then applying all learning in writing in the same text type. The PCMs in this guide will help you to differentiate by offering support in writing tasks. You could also work with a group to use the students' book for guided writing, or to revise language features.

The Literacy Kit

The author team

Geoff Barton is a practising English teacher and Headteacher at King Edward VI School, Bury St Edmunds. He has written a range of popular English course books, and has contributed to the National Strategy training materials.

After two years as Literacy Co-ordinator, and then Basic Skills Co-ordinator, **Michaela Blackledge** took up a post as LEA Literacy Consultant, supporting the KS3 Literacy Pilot in Wakefield schools. She is now Teaching and Learning Manager at Airedale High School, West Yorkshire, and KS3 Learning Manager for the Wakefield Education Action Zone. She was involved in training for the national roll out.

English teacher **Joanna Crewe** is KS3 Strategy Manager and Basic Skills Co-ordinator at Minsthorpe Community College, West Yorkshire.

After a year as Basic Skills Co-ordinator and KS3 Pilot Manager at Minsthorpe Community College, **Jane Flintoft** took up the post of LEA Literacy Consultant in Sheffield. She features on the literacy roll out training video and is now Head of English at Minsthorpe Community College.

Frances Gregory is currently working as a Key Stage 3 Literacy Consultant in West Berkshire. Until April 2001 she was Head of English and Key Stage 3 Strategy Manager at Reading Girls' School which was one of the schools involved in piloting materials prior to the National roll-out.

Jacquie Hills is currently working as a KS3 Literacy Consultant in pilot authority Solihull. She has been involved in training for the national roll out, and has contributed notes on using OHTs for whole class teaching to the training materials. She was Head of English in a 9–13 middle school in Oxford city for seven years, and then a Primary Literacy Consultant in Oxfordshire.

Children's author and editor **Becca Heddle** has contributed to a range of English course books, and has written the model answers in this book.

Using *The Literacy Kit*
Lesson starters

A central component of the KS3 Strategy for English is a lesson structure which begins with a 'starter activity'.

The Literacy Kit Word Level Lesson Starters and *Sentence Level Lesson Starters* boxes provide differentiated resources which can be used in every English classroom. Each contains:

◆ a *Teaching Notes* booklet
◆ a *Photocopy Masters* booklet
◆ bags of word cards in various sizes, labelled by objective number, and in multiple sets where needed
◆ ready-made overhead transparencies
◆ over 100 ideas which can be used straight off the page.

Whole class teaching

Inform, Explain, Describe students' book has a related pack of overhead transparencies (OHTs) containing further texts that inform, explain and describe, and that are taken from a range of literary texts, ICT sources and curriculum areas. The OHTs are designed to be used for whole class teaching of literacy, in shared and modelled reading and writing sessions, and for whole class sentence and word level teaching. Teaching to a text on OHT involves all students during the session and secures their attention by providing them with a single focus, mediated by the teacher. The OHT pack contains a *Teaching Notes* booklet to support teachers in following the teaching sequence advocated in the Strategy. The main focus is on whole class teaching.

Definition of terms for whole class teaching

Shared: the whole class is focused on a piece of text. The focus can be on reading or writing, with the teacher asking for contributions from the students. Shared sessions can also be used for teaching specific points of grammar.

Modelled: this can also be described as 'demonstration'. The teacher makes explicit the process that a reader or writer goes through when reading or writing for a specific process, by 'thinking aloud' and demonstrating the range of strategies that an experienced reader or writer will use automatically. A modelled session is an opportunity to model orally the rehearsals writers make as they compose, revise and edit their work. Towards the end of a modelled writing session, it can be useful to ask students to continue independently or in pairs, for example by drafting out the next sentence. This supports students prior to independent writing. At this point the teacher might highlight effective examples offered by the students, and make assessments about those who may require greater support.

Planning

Each OHT can be used in a number of ways. Teachers may use an OHT text only once, as a brief introduction to a text type or objective. Or they may choose to focus on an OHT over a series of lessons, examining the different features in depth. If teachers are using the *Inform, Explain, Describe* OHTs pack, there will always be a follow-on unit in the students' book for every OHT text, to tie whole class and development sessions together. Linking the focus to the lesson starter as well is an ideal way to make learning focused and explicit, and planning links are given in the notes

Planning and Assessment CD-ROM

This helpful tool brings together the 'Planning links' from all sections of *The Literacy Kit* to help teachers to plan coherent lessons and meet all *Framework* objectives. It also offers support for assessing students' work.

Development

The Literacy Kit students' books are ideal for the independent 'development' session of a literacy lesson. See page 10 for more information, from the author, Geoff Barton.

How to use this *Teacher's Book*

This *Teacher's Book* gives you a brief introduction to the National Strategy, to literacy teaching and to *The Literacy Kit* in general (see pages 5 to 12). However, the main focus of this book is to help teachers in implementing the strategy using *The Literacy Kit* student's book *Inform, Explain, Describe*.

The *Inform, Explain, Describe* students' book, like all three *Literacy Kit* students' books, is ideal for the development section of the literacy lesson and for homework. The texts and questions can of course be used for whole class teaching, but the structure of the book enables students to work independently. (You will find a note from the author of *Inform, Explain, Describe* on page 10 describing how he has used the materials with his own class.) For the busy teacher, this *Teacher's Book* gives the following invaluable support.

Non-fiction text types explained

The structural and grammatical features of different non-fiction text types can seem complex. Adapting the material aimed at the students in *Inform, Explain, Describe*, this section of the *Teacher's Book*, from page 13 onwards, describes in detail typical features of non-fiction text types at text, sentence, and word level, with examples. This description might form the basis of a whole class introduction, could be something the students read independently to revise textual features after shared reading of a text, or could simply be a reminder to teachers of textual features before they begin a unit of work.

This section of the book also introduces the specific text examples used in the students' book, relating them to the features listed above. It then summarizes briefly the objectives that will be taught by working through each unit in the students' book. (More detailed coverage of objectives is given from page 23 on.)

Teaching notes

There is a set of teaching notes for every unit in the students' book, covering the following:

Aim: The notes firstly state the aim of the unit and summarize the objectives to be taught.

Planning links: 'Planning links' give suggestions on how to integrate other parts of *The Literacy Kit* or other resources, for example by suggesting appropriate lesson starters, or linked OHT texts.

Objectives: There is then a very detailed summary of the objectives covered in each unit. Uniquely, objectives are linked to exactly those questions in the students' book that teach them. This approach was taken after consultation with pilot schools who felt there was too much 'learning by osmosis' in some traditional course books – objectives are not cited here that *could* be addressed within a text or unit. Only those that actually *are* addressed by specific teaching or questioning are listed. This enables a detailed record to be kept and also ensures that you can keep a record of gaps in learning if students do not complete all questions in a unit.

Answers: Model answers are given in a separate section, but each set of teaching notes has a handy page reference to help the teacher find the appropriate answers to the unit they are working with.

Photocopy masters: Likewise, PCMs are given in a separate section, but the reference here in the teaching notes makes accessing the appropriate PCMs easy.

Notes to photocopy masters: This paragraph in the teaching notes describes the appropriate PCM/s to use with the unit. In the main, the PCMs are designed to support differentiation, offering ideas or structures to support students in their writing; this section explains how this works.

Answers

This section in the *Teacher's Book* (pages 40–89) offers full, detailed and differentiated model answers to all questions in the students' book (except for writing activities when the answers will be individual to each student or group). The questions from the students' book are repeated, with answers then given in italics.

Photocopy masters

This *Teacher's Book* contains a range of useful PCMs, grouped together at the back of the book. These may be unit-specific, for example writing frames for particular text types. Unit-specific PCMs are numbered by the units to which they are linked. Or they may be more general, such as research sheets. General PCMs are titled as such. Refer to the teaching notes for each unit for notes on how and why each PCM might be used.

The Literacy Kit students' books

Inform, Explain, Describe students' book is a central part of *The Literacy Kit*. It provides the core texts you will need for developing students' reading, writing and spoken work.

You may have used one of the starter activities in the *Lesson Starters* boxes to kick the lesson off, and OHTs to initiate whole class discussion of text types. Now comes the developmental stage, in which students focus on the specific word, sentence and text level objectives of the *Framework*.

The texts

The students' book provides you with texts that are closely mapped to all the objectives and organized on a year-by-year basis, enabling you to plan more carefully and to ensure that essential text types are covered in each year. The *Objectives* box at the head of each text extract details the objectives addressed.

The texts always begin with an *Introduction*. This is a brisk, context-setting starter which tunes students into the type of text they are looking at. It will get them focusing on the language features and issues they can expect to be dealing with. You may want to develop this, asking students to make predictions before they start to read the text.

The texts themselves have been carefully selected to highlight some key features of structure and language, and to match the appropriate levels of interest and ability of students in different year groups. You'll find plenty of texts on contemporary subjects that should appeal to boys and girls aged 11–14.

The questions

The questions which follow provide for two levels of response. *Understanding the text* asks straightforward, fact-spotting questions. Don't underestimate the importance of these: they are the questions that quickly build students' confidence in skimming and scanning, helping them to identify key points quickly.

Interpreting the text offers more open-ended questions. Here students will need to give more reflective responses, often writing short paragraphs explaining and justifying their thoughts.

The *Language and structure* section highlights the new emphasis on language skills within the *Framework*. These are not arid, 'spot the split infinitive' style questions. Their focus is on language in use, getting students to look at writers' language decisions,

catalogue features of the text and then comment on effect. This is the central part of the literacy process – emphasizing effect.

Writing activities

The *Writing activity* focuses on an aspect of the text and encourages students to respond in a more developed way. They may be asked to practise a language skill in greater detail, or to rewrite part of the text in a different style. Importantly, this is the part of the process that shifts the emphasis from reading to writing. Having explored features of the writer's approach in a text, students now begin to write for themselves. It is part of the process of scaffolding writing.

Each unit concludes with an *Extended writing* task. Here the emphasis on developing students' writing skills is consolidated. These are bigger, more ambitious tasks which link back to the texts that students have been exploring. The tasks are scaffolded with suggestions, hints and, often, starter sentences. This approach should help students in the transition from dependent to independent writers.

Speaking and listening

Speaking and listening is integral to all English work and we know that you will be talking to students about their perceptions of texts throughout the process. We have also built in speaking and listening tasks where they develop language skills, or provide an opportunity to meet *Framework* objectives.

The Literacy Kit is, as you can see, a completely integrated scheme. I've been using it with my students here in Suffolk and the response to the variety, the rapid pace, and the sheer range of materials has been terrific – even from my more reluctant students!

I hope it proves similarly enjoyable and useful for you, helping you with the planning and delivery of the *Framework* in a lively and systematic way. Most of all, I hope your students have fun with the huge variety of new resources here.

Your feedback, via the website, is very welcome.

Geoff Barton
www.oup.com/uk/litkit

Management issues

Planning/resourcing

To lighten the burden of resourcing for a department, it makes sense to invest time and energy early on, and build up or purchase a central bank of hard-wearing resources. A successful approach to planning involves working collaboratively; avoid isolated planning to increase efficiency.

Planning using The Literacy Kit

The Literacy Kit provides resources for every objective in the *Framework*, for all the text types required by the National Curriculum, and for every session of the recommended literacy lesson. The resources have all been carefully planned to fit together to provide a complete scheme of work, or a wealth of resources to dip into when filling gaps in your existing scheme of work. See the descriptions of teaching strategies and *Literacy Kit* components on pages 5–10. Every element of *The Literacy Kit* contains 'Planning links' to assist you in building a scheme of work. See the *Teaching Notes* booklets within the *Lesson Starters* boxes and OHT packs, and the teaching notes pages in this book. All the planning links are brought together on the *Planning and Assessment* CD-ROM.

Group work

To achieve maximum results, group work should always be planned. Where possible, groups should be a mix of gender and ability. Regular rotation of groups and the roles people hold within them, e.g. chairperson, is essential. Rotation of students would also help to avoid friendship groups, which usually debate less. Effective strategies which can be used with larger groups include:

Snowball – Pairs discuss an issue, or brainstorm some initial ideas, then double up to fours and continue the process, then into groups of eight in order to compare ideas and to sort out the best or to agree on a course of action. Finally, the whole class is drawn together and spokespersons for each group of eight feed back ideas. This is a useful strategy to promote more public discussion and debate.

Jigsaw – A topic is divided into sections. In 'home' groups of four or five, students allocate a section each, and then regroup into 'expert' groups. In these groups experts work together on their chosen area, then return to original 'home' groups to report back on their area of expertise. The 'home' group is then set a task that requires the students to use the different areas of expertise for a joint outcome. This strategy requires plenty of advance planning, but is a very effective speaking and listening strategy because it ensures the participation of all students.

Envoys – Once groups have carried out a task, one person from each group is selected as an 'envoy' and moves to a new group to discuss what has been thought, decided, or achieved. The envoy then returns to the original group and feeds back. This is an effective way of avoiding tedious and repetitive 'reporting back' sessions. It also puts a 'press' on the envoy's use of language and creates groups of active listeners.

Listening triads – Students work together in groups of three. Each student takes on the role of the talker, questioner, recorder. The talker explains something, or comments on an issue, or expresses opinions. The questioner prompts and seeks clarification. The recorder makes notes and gives a report at the end of the conversation. Next time roles are changed.

Rainbow groups – A way of ensuring that students are regrouped and learn to work with a range of others. After small groups have discussed together, students are given a number or colour. Students with the same number or colour join up – making groups comprising representatives of each original group. In their new group students take turns to report back on their group's work.

Pair talk – Easy to organize even in cramped classrooms. Ideal to promote high levels of participation and to ensure that the discussions are highly focused, especially if allied to tight deadlines. Use in the early stages of learning for students to recall work from a previous lesson, generate questions, work together to plan a piece of writing, or to take turns to tell a story. Use pairs to promote 'response partners' during the drafting process, and to work as reading partners with an unfamiliar text. Ideal for quick-fire reflection and review, and for rehearsal of ideas before presenting them in the whole class.

Pairs to fours – Students work together in pairs – possibly friendship, possibly boy–girl, etc. Each pair then joins up with another pair to explain and compare ideas.

Differentiation

All materials in *The Literacy Kit* are differentiated. In the students' book, *Inform, Explain, Describe*, there are several layers of question. 'Understanding the text' encourages students to read closely, and checks their understanding of what they have read, while 'Interpreting the text' requires a more inferential read. Teachers will know best which suits each group of students. 'Language and structure' focuses on the essential features of the text. Students may find it useful to refer back to the introduction to the unit if they are unclear as to features of non-fiction text types. Every text has a 'mini' writing activity designed to put into practice one or more of the features studied. There is also an opportunity for 'Extended writing' at the end of every unit. Teachers may move more able writers quickly on to extended writing, or may suggest more 'mini-goes' to those who need further consolidation.

The photocopy masters in the Teacher's Book (grouped together at the back of the book) also support differentiation. Some students may need help in structuring their thoughts, or prompts on language and structural features. Refer to the 'Notes to photocopy masters' section in each set of teaching notes, or the 'Notes to the general photocopy masters' section for advice on how to get the most from the PCMS.

Assessment

Guidance on assessment is given on the *Planning and Assessment* CD-ROM.

NON-FICTION TEXT TYPES EXPLAINED

Year 7

Information texts

Purpose and audience

Information texts need to be clear and easy to understand. Their audience might know nothing about a topic and want to learn (for example, 'A Beginner's Guide to Playing the Guitar'); or they may already know something about the topic but need more detail (for example, 'The Advanced Guide to Website Design').

Text level features

Information texts often contain complex information and must present it as clearly as possible. This may mean using a range of **layout features**. You might expect to find:

- headings and subheadings
- short paragraphs
- different font styles, bold and italic print
- bullet points
- diagrams.

The sequence of information is important. The text may start with **general statements**, followed by more **detail** later. **Examples** are often be included.

Sentence level features

Information texts are often written in the **present tense** ('Diet is an important concern ...'). They may use an impersonal style, with the **third person** ('Diet is ...') rather than first or second person ('I think ...' or 'You should ...').

Information texts often use **connectives** to help the reader follow the organization of ideas – for example, *then, so, next.*

Word level features

Information texts may use **technical terms** and complex language if appropriate. Generally these texts use vocabulary which gives facts rather than a lot of description.

Information texts for Year 7 in Inform, Explain, Describe

There are two model information texts for Year 7 in the *Inform, Explain, Describe* students' book. The first is a piece of formal writing, a government-issued information leaflet 'Young Citizen's Passport'.

With this extract we examine a text that gives information in an organized way. These are the objectives students will be studying:

- Word level: connectives
- Sentence level: tense management
- Reading: evaluate sources, identify main ideas, media audiences (how texts are tailored to their audience), print, sound and image, and non-fiction style (how writers match language and organization to their intentions)
- Writing: organize texts appropriately, and present information
- Speaking and listening: recall main points.

The second text is a more informal information leaflet, 'A Guide to Health', produced by a Year 9 student.

This text is an example of information given in an informal, but well-organized, way. These are the objectives students will be studying:

- Word level: personal spelling (recognize and record spelling errors), and word meaning in context
- Sentence level: vary formality
- Reading: locate information, identify main ideas, media audiences (how texts are tailored to their audience), and print, sound and image
- Writing: drafting process (revise and proofread a text), organize texts appropriately, and present information.

Recounts

Purpose and audience

Recounts are texts which tell us about events. They may be designed to inform us (such as, in a history textbook, a description of the build-up to a battle); or they may be more personal – a diary entry or autobiography describing an event in a person's life.

The audience may already be familiar with the topic or writer, or the information may all be new. The writer usually structures his or her ideas in **chronological order**.

Text level features

Because they are usually chronological, most recounts begin with an **opening paragraph** describing the setting or the start of the event; the **last paragraph** is usually about the end of the event or its aftermath. Paragraphs in between use **connectives** to link the sequence of ideas together.

Sentence level features

Recounts may use the **first person** (for stories and autobiography) or **third person** (for factual reports).

They usually use the **past tense**. There may be a variety of **sentence types** to hold the reader's interest. Short sentences may be used to build tension or suspense. Sometimes a writer uses **dialogue** to move the recount forward or tell us more about a character.

Word level features

Recounts often aim to answer the questions: *who?, what?, when?, where?, why?* Writers paint pictures with words, so we may find descriptive writing, with techniques such as **similes** and **metaphors** used to create vivid images. Writers' choice of words may include the simple or complex, the formal or informal, depending on what they are aiming to achieve.

Recounts for Year 7 in Inform, Explain, Describe

There are two types of model recounts for Year 7 in *Inform, Explain, Describe*. The first is a piece of autobiographical writing, 'Millvina Dean, Survivor of the Titanic'. The writer has adopted some of the characteristics of recounts, but this is a highly personal piece of writing.

With this extract, we will focus on the features of a personal recount, written informally. Students will study these objectives:

- Word level: connectives
- Sentence level: tense management, sentence variety, and vary formality
- Reading: evaluate sources, identify main ideas, infer and deduce (understand implied meanings from evidence in the text), and language choices (how they enhance meanings)
- Writing: drafting process (planning and writing), organize texts appropriately, present information, and evocative description.

The second group of texts comprises four personal recounts on the same subject: 'My First Day at School'.

With these extracts we look at a variety of brief personal recounts, presented informally. Students will study these objectives:

- Word level: connectives
- Sentence level: subordinate clauses, tense management, starting paragraphs, main point of paragraph, and sequencing paragraphs
- Reading: extract information, note-making, active reading, and identify main ideas
- Writing: planning formats, organize texts appropriately, present information, and evocative description

- Speaking and listening: recount, and answer pertinent questions.

Explanation texts
Purpose and audience

Explanation texts aim to help us understand the world. They may explain how something works, or why things are the way they are. They are often aimed at readers who have a particular interest in the topic, or who know a little and wish to know more. It is therefore essential that these texts are clearly written and presented.

Text level features

The layout of these texts is often designed to help them get their explanations across to the reader. This might mean the use of **question and answer** formats, or **short paragraphs**, **bullet-points** and **checklists**. Ideas may be structured in a **step-by-step** way, so that readers build their understanding logically. The steps may even be **numbered** to make the sequence clear.

Sentence level features

These texts are usually written in the **present tense** – explaining how things are now (except where they are explaining an event from history). They might use the **active voice** (e.g. 'The scientist then places the magnesium in the dish …') or the **passive voice**, where the person doing the action is less important than what is done (e.g. 'The magnesium is then placed in the dish …'). The last part of the text might be a **summary**.

Word level features

The writer might include **specialist language**, depending on a) the topic and b) the audience. A glossary may be included to help explain any technical terms. The writing will usually be **direct** and **impersonal**, with little description, so that the essential facts are as clear as possible.

Explanation texts for Year 7 in Inform, Explain, Describe

The model explanation texts in *Inform, Explain, Describe* are both on the same subject, 'Mobile Phones', and are to be compared.

They both aim to explain the same type of information. These are the objectives students will be studying:

- Word level: connectives
- Sentence level: starting paragraphs, paragraph structure, sequencing paragraphs, and vary formality

◆ Reading: compare presentation, evaluate sources, identify main ideas, media audiences (how texts are tailored to their audience), and non-fiction style (how writers match language and organization to their intentions

◆ Writing: drafting process (planning and writing), organize texts appropriately, and develop logic.

Instruction texts

Purpose and audience

Instructions show the reader how to do something, usually in a sequence of steps. The level of detail in instructions will depend on how much the reader already knows. A 'Beginner's Guide to the Internet' may contain more general information than a specialist guide, such as 'Programming in HTML'.

Text level features

The **layout** is often carefully designed to help the reader follow instructions – clarity is essential. **Diagrams** may also be used to show how to do something. The text is structured in a **logical order** and, to make it even clearer, points may be **numbered** in sequence. The writer might also add reassuring comments, or tips, to help the reader: 'Three quick steps to a delicious pudding …'. 'If this seems time-consuming, don't worry – it will be worth it.'

Sentence level features

Sentences will often be **imperatives** (commands), with the verb near the beginning:

*First **take** an egg. **Boil** it.*

Sentences will often address the reader **directly**: 'If you need to check this . . .'. They will often be **short**, so that they are simple to follow, and will use **connectives** to link ideas together, such as *next*, *then*, *now*.

Word level features

Vocabulary is often **plain** and straightforward, except where the intended reader is already an expert in the topic, and may include technical words. There is little use of adjectives, adverbs and imagery: the writer is aiming at clear instructional writing rather than using too much descriptive detail.

Instructional text for Year 7 in Inform, Explain, Describe

The model instructional text in *Inform, Explain, Describe* is called 'Telepathic Powers'.

This extract contains a straightforward set of instructions. These are the objectives students will be studying:

◆ Sentence level: active or passive voice, sequencing paragraphs, vary formality, and speech and writing, (investigating their differences)

◆ Reading: locate information, active reading, identify main ideas, and non-fiction style

◆ Writing: organize texts appropriately, present information, and instructions and directions

◆ Speaking and listening: answers, instructions, explanations, and oral text types (how spoken texts are organized)

Descriptive texts

Purpose and audience

Descriptive texts aim to give us detail. In a brochure, we might get a description of a product. Both fiction and non-fiction writers use descriptive writing to help us to visualize people or places. The level of description used will depend on the writer's aims. A short story may contain a brief but vivid description of a character; a film review may give a detailed description of the way a film is structured.

Text level features

These texts may begin with general **opening statements** (e.g. 'I remember my own schooldays') and then move into a series of descriptive sentences which add **detail** rather than new points. Nouns and verbs will often be modified by **adjectives** and **adverbs** (e.g. 'the *reddish* bricks', 'walking *painfully*').

Sentence level features

Descriptive texts may be in the **third person**, particularly in advertising and reviews; or they may use the **first person**, especially in autobiographical writing and some stories. The **tense** will vary too. Descriptions are often in the present tense ('Ickworth Park is glorious in the spring'), except in fiction and autobiographical writing ('The school buildings looked large and threatening'). Sentences may be longer because they use **modification** – adjectives and adverbs – to add detail.

Word level features

Vocabulary is **precise** and **vivid**. There may be **figurative language** (such as the use of similes and metaphors) in order to help the reader visualize what is being described. The writer may use **technical words** in some contexts (a brochure about a new car, for example). Connectives such as *and*, *also*, *similarly* are used to link ideas together.

Descriptive text for Year 7 in Inform, Explain, Describe

The model descriptive text in *Inform, Explain, Describe* is a description of a place, called 'Memories of Leeds'.

This extract is an example of vivid description. Students will be studying the following objectives:

◆ Sentence level: subordinate clauses
◆ Reading: active reading, infer and deduce (understand implied meanings from evidence in the text), character, setting and mood, and language choices (how they enhance meanings)
◆ Writing: present information, and evocative description.

Year 8

Recounts

Purpose and audience

Recounts tell us about events. They include:

- autobiographies
- stories from history
- someone describing a crime they have just witnessed
- a newspaper story.

The audience may be familiar with the topic or writer, or it may all be new. The events will usually be retold in **chronological order**.

Text level features

Most recounts begin with an **opening paragraph** to set the scene, then give a description of events, and end with a **concluding paragraph**. Paragraphs use **connectives** to link the sequence of ideas together.

Sentence level features

Recounts usually use the **first person** (for stories and autobiography) or the **third person** (for factual reports). They are usually written in the **past tense**.

Often, there is a variety of **sentence types** to create interest (e.g. several short sentences to build up suspense). Sometimes **dialogue** is used to move the recount forward or to tell us more about a character.

Word level features

Recounts often aim to answer the questions: *who?*, *where?*, *when?*, *what?*, *why?* They may include descriptive writing, and techniques like **simile** and **metaphor** to create more vivid images. They may use words which are simple or complex, formal or informal, depending on what the writer is aiming to achieve.

Recounts for Year 8 in Inform, Explain, Describe

There are two types of recount for Year 8 in the *Inform, Explain, Describe* students' book. The first is a newspaper report from the *Sun* called 'Flying Solo'. It is a typical example of traditional news reporting.

This extract is an informal, entertaining newspaper report. Students will study the following objectives:

- Word level: formality and word choice
- Sentence level: complex sentences, variety of sentence structure, full range of punctuation, adapting text types, and degrees of formality

- Reading: note-making formats, implied and explicit meanings, and development of key ideas
- Writing: anticipate reader reaction, effective information, explain complex ideas, and formal description
- Speaking and listening: commentary, and listen for a specific purpose.

The second text is an entertaining personal recount by Bill Bryson, 'Going Surfing'.

Using comic effects in a recount is an important way of entertaining the reader, as this extract shows. These are the objectives students will study:

- Word level: formality and word choice, and ironic use of words
- Sentence level: variety of sentence structure, adapting text types, and degrees of formality
- Reading: implied and explicit meanings, and transposition (how meanings are changed when information is presented in different forms)
- Writing: establish the tone, effective information, and formal description.

Autobiographical recounts

Purpose and audience

Recounts tell readers about events that have happened. We have already seen them in newspapers and in personal accounts.

Autobiographies are important examples of recounts. They describe the events that have taken place in someone's own life. Usually, they aim to entertain the reader.

Text level features

Most autobiography is written in a **chronological** sequence.

It is important to remember, however, that autobiographies often reflect the **personality** of the writer: they might change the conventions or rules of writing to suit themselves. For example, in his autobiography *Timebends*, the playwright Arthur Miller does not use a chronological sequence. Instead, he moves backwards and forwards over events in his life.

Sentence level features

Autobiographies use the **first person** ('I' and 'me'). They aim to paint a picture with words in order to help the reader visualize the scenes and events from the writer's life. **Connectives** like *then*, *later*, *next* are used to link the ideas together and show the movement of time.

Word level features

Autobiographical writing often uses descriptive language, and techniques such as **similes** and **metaphors**. It usually aims to answer the questions *who?*, *what?*, *where?*, *when?*, *why?*

Autobiographical recounts for Year 8 in Inform, Explain, Describe

There are two autobiographical recounts for Year 8 in *Inform, Explain, Describe*. The first is a piece by James Herriott called 'Healing the Horses'.

In this extract, the writer gives an account of his own experiences in a form that reads like a novel. Students will learn about the following objectives:

- Word level: unfamiliar words (working out their meaning), and formality and word choice
- Sentence level: adapting text types, and standard English and dialect
- Reading: note-making formats, versatile reading (using a range of reading strategies), and transposition (how meanings are changed when information is presented in different forms)
- Writing: effective planning, effective information, and formal description.

The second extract is a personal recount by the singer Des'ree called 'Relative Values'. It is about her childhood and her relationship with her parents.

This extract gives a very personal view of a period in the writer's life. These are the objectives students will be studying:

- Word level: prepositions and connectives, and formality and word choice
- Sentence level: variety of sentence structure, colons and semi-colons, grouping sentences, and cohesion and coherence
- Reading: trace developments (of themes and values), and bias and objectivity
- Writing: effective information, and formal description.

Information texts

Purpose and audience

Information texts describe how things are. They include reference books, dictionaries, textbooks, factsheets, and leaflets.

The audience will be people who want to know more about the topic. They may already have some knowledge of the subject.

Information texts should be clear, well-ordered, and easy to follow.

Text level features

Information texts often use **headings** to break the information up into different sections, and use **layout features** such as tables and diagrams to help make the information clear.

They might start with **general facts** and then go into more **detail**. Often they use a **non-chronological order** – they place information in order of importance, not the order that events take place.

Sentence level features

Information texts usually use:

- the **third-person**, to create an impersonal tone
- the **present tense**
- the **passive voice** ('salmon are farmed in large tanks' rather than 'people farm salmon in large tanks')
- a mix of **simple and compound sentences**
- questions addressed to the reader, to involve the reader more.

Word level features

Information texts often use precise terms, and sometimes **technical language**. This will depend on how much the writer thinks the reader knows about the topic. The writers of information texts avoid using much descriptive language. They emphasize **facts**, using nouns and verbs in order to describe processes, and the text is usually formal.

Information text for Year 8 in Inform, Explain, Describe

The model information text for Year 8 in *Inform, Explain, Describe* is called 'Exploded Drawings'.

This extract explains some technical information and uses specialist vocabulary. These are the objectives students will be studying:

- Word level: unfamiliar words (working out their meaning), words in context, specialist vocabulary, and formality and word choice
- Sentence level: variety of sentence structure, grouping sentences, subject-specific conventions, and degrees of formality
- Reading: versatile reading (using a range of reading strategies), transposition (how meanings are changed when information is presented in different forms) and development of key ideas
- Writing: effective information, explain complex ideas, and formal description
- Speaking and listening: listen for a specific purpose.

Explanation texts

Purpose and audience

Explanation texts explain how things work and why things happen. They give us the answers to questions (such as 'Why did war break out in 1914?') and they are usually clear and direct.

Text level features

Explanation texts often:

- use **layout features** to make their explanation clearer (e.g. questions, subheadings, boxes, illustrations, diagrams, maps)
- begin with a general **opening statement** ('Europe in 1914 was on the brink of war …')
- give a **step-by-step** account of an event or process
- end with a **summary**.

Sentence level features

Explanation texts usually:

- use the **third-person** to create an impersonal tone

- use the **present tense** (in science and technical writing, for example) or the **past tense** (for historical writing)
- make some use of the **passive voice** to keep the tone impersonal ('the potassium was then added to the solution')
- use a mix of **simple and compound sentences**
- use **connectives** to show how one idea relates to another and to indicate cause and effect (e.g. *after, until, later*).

Word level features

Explanation texts often use precise terms, and sometimes **technical language**. This will depend on how much the writer thinks the reader knows about the topic. Explanation texts usually avoid using much descriptive language – they emphasize **facts**. They use nouns and verbs in order to describe processes.

Explanation text for Year 8 in Inform, Explain, Describe

The model explanation text for Year 8 in *Inform, Explain, Describe* is taken from the BBC Science Shack website. It explains why the sky is blue most of the time but can be red at sunrise and sunset.

This website page gives an easy-to-follow explanation of what is happening during a process. These are the objectives students will be studying:

- Word level: words in context, prepositions and connectives, and formality and word choice
- Sentence level: tense shifts, conditionals and modal verbs, subject-specific conventions, and informal to formal (identifying the alterations made to change a text from informal to formal)
- Reading: development of key ideas
- Writing: effective information.

Year 9

Media recounts

Introduction

Earlier units in the *Inform, Explain, Describe* students' book looked at several different types of recount:

- personal recounts ('My First Day at School', page 18)
- newspaper recounts ('Flying Solo', page 44)
- recounts to entertain ('Going Surfing', page 50)
- autobiography (James Herriott, page 58 and Des'ree, page 64).

These showed that recounts:

- may include autobiography, newspaper articles, reports, and historical texts
- aim to inform and entertain
- are usually structured in **chronological order**
- may use the **first person** (autobiography) or the **third person** (history)
- aim to paint pictures in words, so they may use plenty of **description**.

Newspaper recounts

This unit focuses on the types of recount found in the media, and how they use description.

Newspapers use their front page to inform readers about the stories that seem most important. They then sometimes include further articles on the same topic later in the newspaper, or on a later date. Here the purpose might be to provide more detailed information or different viewpoints. Our first extract is of this type.

Newspapers also investigate events that are not major news – mysteries, amusing stories, or local events. The second extract in this unit is an example of this type of article.

Media recounts for Year 9 in Inform, Explain, Describe

There are two media recounts for Year 9 in the *Inform, Explain, Describe* students' book. The first is a newspaper article about a raid at the Millennium Dome, 'An Ealing Comedy of Errors'.

This extract gives newspaper readers the facts about a news event. These are the objectives students will be studying:

- Word level: layers of meaning
- Sentence level: degrees of formality, integrate speech, reference and quotation, and paragraph organization

- Reading: evaluate information, readers and texts (how they influence each other), author's standpoint, and rhetorical devices
- Writing: 'infotainment' (how information texts can be amusing and entertaining), and descriptive detail.

The second recount is a newspaper investigation entitled 'The Lancashire Cat Mystery'.

This extract treats an unusual event in an original way. Students will be studying these objectives:

- Word level: connectives for developing thought
- Sentence level: degrees of formality, integrate speech, reference and quotation, and paragraph organization
- Reading: evaluate information, readers and texts (how they influence each other), author's standpoint, and rhetorical devices
- Writing: creativity in non-literary texts, 'infotainment' (how information texts can be amusing and entertaining), and descriptive detail.

Travel writing

Introduction

Travel writing is a form of recount that shows us people and places through the eyes of the writer. Often the setting is exotic, although writers might also describe places nearer to home – for example, another famous traveller, Eric Newby, described the exciting memories he had of travelling through Harrods, the London department store.

Travel writing:

- reports on the experiences of going to places and meeting people
- may aim to inform as well as entertain us
- is usually retold in **chronological order**
- usually uses the **first person**
- aims to paint pictures in words, so it may use plenty of **descriptive language**.

Travel writing for Year 9 in Inform, Explain, Describe

There are two examples of travel writing for Year 9 in *Inform, Explain, Describe*. The first is 'Sinking Fast', an extract from a book by the American yachtsman, Steve Callahan.

This extract is a dramatic and entertaining recount of an incident that took place on a journey. Students will be studying the following objectives:

- Word level: terminology for analysis (using appropriate terms for analysing language), and layers of meaning
- Sentence level: complex sentences, and punctuation for clarity and effect
- Reading: rhetorical devices
- Writing: 'infotainment' (how information texts can be amusing and entertaining), integrate information, and descriptive detail.

The second text is a description of a storm in the Sahara called 'A Desert Dies'.

This extract gives a highly descriptive recount of the traveller's experiences. These are the objectives students will study:

- Word level: layers of meaning
- Sentence level: degrees of formality
- Reading: note-making at speed, and rhetorical devices
- Writing: creativity in non-literary texts, and integrate information.

Information texts to persuade
Introduction

So far we have looked at several information texts:

- Young Citizen's Passport (page 2)
- A Guide to Health (page 6)
- Exploded Drawings (page 72).

This unit focuses on the way information texts can also combine elements of instruction and persuasion. They give information, but this is then used as a source of advice.

Information texts describe how things are. They are written for an audience who will usually want to know more about the topic, but may already have some knowledge of the subject.

Information texts are clear, well-ordered, and easy to follow, often using **layout features** such as tables and diagrams to help make the information clear. They usually place information in **order of importance**, not chronological order.

Usually they use the **third-person** to create an impersonal tone, and the **present tense**. Often they use very precise terms, and sometimes **technical language**. The level of technical language will depend

on how much the writer thinks the reader already knows about the topic.

Information texts avoid using much descriptive language. They emphasize **facts**.

Information texts to persuade for Year 9 in Inform, Explain, Describe

The model information texts for Year 9 in *Inform, Explain, Describe* are both about 'Choosing to Be Vegetarian'.

Here we compare two examples of information texts that intend to persuade their audience to do something: a leaflet and a web page. Students will be studying the following objectives:

- Word level: apply knowledge (of word origins), and connectives for developing thought
- Sentence level: paragraph organization, and conventions of ICT texts
- Reading: synthesize information (put it together from different sources), evaluate information, compare texts, and author's standpoint
- Writing: presentational devices, integrate information, explain connections, and effective presentation of information.

Explanations
Introduction

We have looked at some explanation texts already in *Inform, Explain, Describe*:

- Mobile Phones (page 24)
- Why is the sky blue…? (page 80)

Explanation texts aim to explain how things work, why things happen, and to give us answers to questions.

They are usually clear and direct, and often begin with a general **opening statement**, then give a **step-by-step** account of an event or process. They often end with a **summary**.

Explanations usually use the **third person** and the **present tense**, but for writing about past events (historical writing) they will use the **past tense**.

Connectives are used to show how one idea relates to another and to indicate cause and effect.

Very precise terms, and sometimes **technical language**, are used in explanation texts, depending on how much the reader is likely to know about the topic.

Explanation texts emphasize **facts and causes**, and do not use much descriptive language.

Explanation for Year 9 in Inform, Explain, Describe

The model explanation text for Year 9 in *Inform, Explain, Describe* is a school worksheet for history students called 'Tollund Man'.

This extract explains the results of a scientific investigation. These are the objectives students will be studying:

◆ Word level: connectives for developing thought
◆ Sentence level: degrees of formality, paragraph organization, and sustained standard English
◆ Reading: information retrieval
◆ Writing: review own writing, exploratory writing, formal essay, narrative techniques, and explain connections.

Playing with non-fiction conventions
Introduction

Once students become familiar with the way different non-fiction texts are written, it can be entertaining to play around with the conventions and rules.

A lot of comedy shows and films do this kind of thing. For example, the 'Airplane' movies took the conventions of disaster films and made them funny; comedy programmes like 'The Fast Show' imitate news or documentary programmes.

Poking fun at a style of text or programme in this creative way is known as **parody**. This unit looks at one specific example of a parody – the way the magazine *Private Eye* uses the conventions of a newspaper to retell some parts of the story of *Macbeth*.

Parodies often use the conventions of a well-known type of text (e.g. news bulletins, documentaries, newspaper reports) and apply them to unexpected subject matter.

Playing with non-fiction conventions for Year 9 in Inform, Explain, Describe

The text for playing with non-fiction conventions for Year 9 in *Inform, Explain, Describe* is a parody from the satirical magazine *Private Eye*.

This extract takes the events of a Shakespeare play (*Macbeth*) and creates a parody of a newspaper report about politicians. Students will be studying these objectives:

◆ Word level: layers of meaning
◆ Sentence level: exploit conventions
◆ Reading: readers and texts (how they influence each other), and author's standpoint
◆ Writing: 'infotainment' (how information texts can be amusing and entertaining), and descriptive detail.

Teaching Notes

Year 7 units

Unit 1 Information texts

Young Citizen's Passport

With this extract we examine a text that gives information in an organized way. These are the objectives students will be studying:

- Word level: connectives
- Sentence level: tense management
- Reading: evaluate sources, identify main ideas, media audiences (how texts are tailored to their audience), print, sound and image, and non-fiction style (how writers match language and organization to their intentions)
- Writing: organize texts appropriately, and present information
- Speaking and listening: recall main points.

A Guide to Health

This text is an example of information given in an informal, but well-organized, way. These are the objectives students will be studying:

- Word level: personal spelling (recognize and record spelling errors), and word meaning in context
- Sentence level: vary formality
- Reading: locate information, identify main ideas, media audiences (how texts are tailored to their audience), and print, sound and image
- Writing: drafting process (revise and proofread a text), organize texts appropriately, and present information.

Planning links

See Unit 1 of *The Literacy Kit Inform, Explain, Describe Overhead Transparencies Pack* for information texts for whole class work.

Further and more challenging information texts are provided throughout the Inform, *Explain, Describe* strand.

For ready-made lesson starters for all word and sentence level objectives, including those taught in this Unit, see *The Literacy Kit Word* and *Sentence Level Lesson Starters* boxes.

Objectives taught in this unit

Extended Writing reinforces objectives taught throughout the unit, plus Writing 2 Planning formats, and Speaking and listening 6 Recall main points

Young Citizen's Passport

Word level

20 Connectives (Language and structure 3, p. 4)

Sentence level

4 Tense management (Language and structure 2, p. 4; Writing activity, p. 5)

13a Information (Language and structure 1–4, p. 4; Writing activity, p. 5)

Reading

5 Evaluate sources (Interpreting the text 6, p. 4)

7 Identify main ideas (Understanding the text 1–4, p. 3; Language and structure 4, p. 5)

10 Media audiences (Interpreting the text 5, 6, p. 4)

11 Print, sound and image (Interpreting the text 5, p. 4)

13 Non-fiction style (Interpreting the text 5, 6, p. 4; Language and structure 1–4, pp. 4–5)

Writing

10 Organize texts appropriately (Writing activity, p. 5)

11 Present information (Writing activity, p. 5)

Speaking and listening

6 Recall main points (Understanding the text 1–4, p. 3 if text is read aloud first)

A Guide to Health

Word level

8 Personal spelling (Language and structure 5, p. 9)

14 Word meaning in context (Understanding the text 4, p. 6)

Sentence level

13a Information (Language and structure 1–3, p. 8; Language and structure 4, 6, p. 9)

15 Vary formality (Interpreting the text 7, p. 8; Writing activity, p. 9)

Reading

1 Locate information (Understanding the text 1–4, p. 6; Interpreting the text 5, p. 8)

7 Identify main ideas (Interpreting the text 5, p. 8)

10 Media audiences (Interpreting the text 7, p. 8; Language and structure 3, p. 8)

11 Print, sound and image (Interpreting the text 6, p. 8; Language and structure 6, p. 9)

Writing

1 Drafting process (Writing activity, p. 9)

10 Organize texts appropriately (Writing activity, p. 9)

11 Present information (Writing activity, p. 9)

Answers

Answers to this unit are provided on page 40 onwards.

Photocopy master

A photocopy master for this unit is provided at the back of this book – see Unit 1 PCM A. See also General PCMs 1 – Brainstorming and 5 – Information.

Notes to the photocopy master

Unit 1 PCM A – Healthy eating (Writing activity, p. 9)

This is a frame to assist students in the writing activity where they are asked to present the information included in Nick Vollmer's leaflet in a more formal, impersonal way. Tips on how to make the leaflet more formal have been included, e.g. don't shorten words – 'carbohydrates', not 'carbs'. In addition, there are four boxes with prompts to help students structure the facts for the leaflet.

Unit 2 Recounts

Millvina Dean, Survivor of the Titanic

With this extract we focus on the features of a personal recount, written informally. Students will study these objectives:

◆ Word level: connectives
◆ Sentence level: tense management, sentence variety, and vary formality
◆ Reading: evaluate sources, identify main ideas, infer and deduce (understand implied meanings from evidence in the text), and language choices (how they enhance meanings)
◆ Writing: drafting process (planning and writing), organize texts appropriately, present information, and evocative description.

My First Day at School

With these extracts we look at a variety of brief personal recounts, presented informally. Students will study these objectives:

◆ Word level: connectives
◆ Sentence level: subordinate clauses, tense management, starting paragraphs, main point of paragraph, and sequencing paragraphs
◆ Reading: extract information, note-making, active reading, and identify main ideas
◆ Writing: planning formats, organize texts appropriately, present information, and evocative description

◆ Speaking and listening: recount, and pertinent questions.

Planning links

See Unit 2 of *The Literacy Kit Inform, Explain, Describe Overhead Transparencies Pack* for recount texts for whole class work.

Further and more challenging recount texts are provided throughout the *Inform, Explain, Describe* strand.

For ready-made lesson starters for all word and sentence level objectives, including those taught in this Unit, see *The Literacy Kit Word* and *Sentence Level Lesson Starters* boxes.

Objectives taught in this unit

Extended writing reinforces objectives taught throughout the unit.

Millvina Dean, Survivor of the Titanic

Word level

20 Connectives (Language and structure 4, p. 15; Writing activity, p. 16)

Sentence level

4 Tense management (Language and structure 5, p. 15; Writing activity, p. 16)

11 Sentence variety (Language and structure 3, p. 15; Writing activity, p. 16)

13b Recount (Language and structure 3, 5, p. 15; Language and structure 6, p. 16)

15 Vary formality (Language and structure 2, p. 15; Writing activity, p. 16)

Reading

5 Evaluate sources (Interpreting the text 7, p. 14; Language and structure 7, p. 16)

7 Identify main ideas (Understanding the text 6, p. 14)

8 Infer and deduce (Interpreting the text 8, 9, p. 14)

14 Language choices (Language and structure 1–3, pp. 14–15)

Writing

1 Drafting process (Writing activity, p. 16)

10 Organize texts appropriately (Writing activity, p. 16)

11 Present information (Writing activity, p. 16)

14 Evocative description (Writing activity, p. 16)

My First Day at School

Word level

20 Connectives (Writing activity, p. 21)

Sentence level

1 Subordinate clauses (Language and structure 1, p. 20)

4 Tense management (Language and structure 2, p. 21; Writing activity, p. 21)

8 Starting paragraphs (Language and structure 1, p. 20)

9 Main point of paragraph (Language and structure 1, p. 20)

12 Sequencing paragraphs (Language and structure 1, p. 20; Writing activity, p. 21)

13b Recount (Language and structure 1, 2, pp. 20–1; Writing activity, p. 21)

Reading

2 Extract information (Understanding the text 1, 2, p. 20; Interpreting the text 3–5, p. 20)

4 Note-making (Understanding the text 1, p. 20)

6 Active reading (Interpreting the text 3–5, p. 20)

7 Identify main ideas (Understanding the text 1, p. 20; Language and structure 1, p. 20)

Writing

2 Planning formats (Understanding the text 1, p. 20)

10 Organize texts appropriately (Writing activity, p. 21)

11 Present information (Writing activity, p. 21)

14 Evocative description (Writing activity, p. 21)

Speaking and listening

2 Recount (Writing activity, p. 21)

7 Pertinent questions (Writing activity, p. 21)

Answers

Answers to this unit are provided on page 44 onwards.

Photocopy masters

Photocopy masters for this unit are provided at the back of this book – see Unit 2 PCMs A and B. See also General PCM 6 – Recount.

Notes to the photocopy masters

Unit 2 PCM A – My first day at school (Understanding the text 1, p. 20)

This is a grid that provides students with a scaffold for their research on what each of the famous people recalls about their first day at school. Boxes are headed: 'Name', 'Best known as' and 'Main points'. The main points boxes include three bullet points to help students structure their research. They will have to be concise to fit the information into the boxes, and this should encourage them to read and summarize it rather than just copying out huge chunks.

Unit 2 PCM B – My first day at school (Extended writing, p. 22)

This is a bank of sentence starters to help students structure their recount about their first day at school. The sentence prompts have been divided into three sections: 'Beginning', 'Middle' and 'End' to give students support throughout the task. The bank will enable them to select appropriate 'sentence starters' for their recount and will also familiarize them with alternatives that they may use in future writing tasks. Various connectives have been included to encourage students to sequence their writing chronologically.

Unit 3 Explanation texts

Mobile Phones

Both texts aim to explain the same type of information. These are the objectives students will be studying:

◆ Word level: connectives
◆ Sentence level: starting paragraphs, paragraph structure, sequencing paragraphs, and vary formality
◆ Reading: compare presentation, evaluate sources, identify main ideas, media audiences (how texts are tailored to their audience), and non-fiction style (how writers match language and organization to their intentions)
◆ Writing: drafting process (planning and writing), organize texts appropriately, and develop logic.

Planning links

See Unit 3 of *The Literacy Kit Inform, Explain, Describe Overhead Transparencies Pack* for an explanation text for whole class work.

Further and more challenging explanation texts are provided throughout the *Inform, Explain, Describe* strand.

For ready-made lesson starters for all word and sentence level objectives, including those taught in this Unit, see *The Literacy Kit Word* and *Sentence Level Lesson Starters* boxes.

Objectives taught in this unit

Extended writing reinforces objectives taught throughout the unit, plus Sentence level 14 Subject conventions.

Word level

20 Connectives (Interpreting the text 12, p. 27; Writing activity, p. 28)

Sentence level

8 Starting paragraphs (Language and structure 4, p. 27)

10 Paragraph structure (Writing activity, p. 28)

12 Sequencing paragraphs (Interpreting the text 12, p. 27; Language and structure 2–4, p. 27; Writing activity, p. 28)

13c Explanation (Understanding the text 9, p. 26; Interpreting the text 12, p. 27; Language and structure 2–4, p. 27; Writing activity, p. 28)

15 Vary formality (Language and structure 1, 3, p. 27; Language and structure 5, p. 28)

Reading

3 Compare presentation (Understanding the text 9, p. 26; Interpreting the text 10, 11, p. 26; Language and structure 2, 3, p. 27)

5 Evaluate sources (Interpreting the text 12, p. 27)

7 Identify main ideas (Understanding the text 1–8, p. 26)

10 Media audiences (Language and structure 2, 3, p. 27)

13 Non-fiction style (Understanding the text 9, p. 26; Interpreting the text 12, p. 27; Language and structure 1–5, pp. 27–8)

Writing

1 Drafting process (Writing activity, p. 28)

10 Organize texts appropriately (Writing activity, p. 28)

12 Develop logic (Writing activity, p. 28)

Answers

Answers to this unit are provided on page 49 onwards.

Photocopy master

A photocopy master for this unit is provided at the back of this book – see Unit 3 PCM A. See also General PCM 7 – Explanation, and 1 – Brainstorming.

Notes to photocopy master

Unit 3 PCM A – Similarities and differences (interpreting the text 10 and 11, p. 26)

This is a sheet that provides students with pointers on what to look for in the two texts to get them started on their analysis, e.g. How do the texts begin? The two boxes ask students to list similarities between the texts, and to identify the differences. Each box contains six bullet points to help students structure their findings.

Unit 4 Instruction texts

Telepathic Powers

This extract contains a straightforward set of instructions. These are the objectives students will be studying:

- ◆ Sentence level: active or passive voice, sequencing paragraphs, vary formality, and speech and writing (investigating their differences)
- ◆ Reading: locate information, active reading, identify main ideas, and non-fiction style
- ◆ Writing: organize texts appropriately, present information, and instructions and directions
- ◆ Speaking and listening: answers, instructions, explanations, and oral text types (how spoken texts are organized).

Planning links

See Unit 4 of *The Literacy Kit Inform, Explain, Describe Overhead Transparencies Pack* for an instructional text for whole class work.

For ready-made lesson starters for all word and sentence level objectives, including those taught in this Unit, see *The Literacy Kit Word* and *Sentence Level Lesson Starters* boxes.

Objectives taught in this unit

Extended writing reinforces objectives taught throughout the unit.

Sentence level

5 Active or passive voice (Language and structure 2a, p. 34)

12 Sequencing paragraphs (Language and structure 3, p. 35)

13d Instructions (Understanding the text 4, p. 33; Interpreting the text 9, 10, p. 34; Language and structure 1–3, pp. 34–5)

15 Vary formality (Language and structure 2b, p. 34; Language and structure 3, p. 35)

16 Speech and writing (Language and structure 3, p. 35)

Reading

1 Locate information (Understanding the text 6, 7, p. 34)

6 Active reading (Understanding the text 4, 5, pp. 33–4)

7 Identify main ideas (Understanding the text 6, 7, p. 34)

13 Non-fiction style (Interpreting the text 9, p. 34; Language and structure 1, 2, p. 34)

Writing

10 Organize texts appropriately (Writing activity, p. 35)

11 Present information (Writing activity, p. 35)

13 Instructions and directions (Writing activity, p. 35)

Speaking and listening

4 Answers, instructions, explanations (Language and structure 3, p. 35)

9 Oral text types (Language and structure 3, p. 35)

Answers

Answers to this unit are provided on page 52 onwards.

Notes to photocopy master

General PCM 10 Instruction texts is ideal for use with this unit. It offers a frame to support the writing of instructional texts, and will enable students to remember key organizational and stylistic features of this text type. It can be used as a planning, drafting or writing frame.

Unit 5 Descriptive texts

Memories of Leeds

This extract is an example of vivid description. Students will be studying the following objectives:

- Sentence level: subordinate clauses
- Reading: active reading, infer and deduce (understand implied meanings from evidence in the text), character, setting and mood, and language choices (how they enhance meanings)
- Writing: present information, and evocative description

Planning links

See Unit 5 of *The Literacy Kit Inform, Explain, Describe Overhead Transparencies Pack* for descriptive texts for whole class work.

Descriptive writing also features in *The Literacy Kit Imagine, Explore, Entertain* strand.

For ready-made lesson starters for all word and sentence level objectives, including those taught in this Unit, see *The Literacy Kit Word* and *Sentence Level Lesson Starters* boxes.

Objectives taught in this unit

Extended writing reinforces objectives taught throughout the unit, plus Speaking and listening 7 Pertinent questions.

Sentence level

1 Subordinate clauses (Language and structure 3, p. 40)

Reading

6 Active reading (Understanding the text 5, p. 39; Interpreting the text 6, p. 40; Language and structure 5, p. 41)

8 Infer and deduce (Understanding the text 5, p. 39; Interpreting the text 6, p. 40)

12 Character, setting and mood (Language and structure 1–6, pp. 40–1)

14 Language choices (Language and structure 1–6, pp. 40–1)

Writing

11 Present information (Writing activity, p. 41)

14 Evocative description (Writing activity, p. 41)

Answers

Answers to this unit are provided on page 54 onwards.

Photocopy master

A photocopy master for this unit is provided at the back of this book – see Unit 5 PCM A.

Notes to photocopy master

Unit 5 PCM A – Planning a description (Extended writing, p. 42)

This is a frame consisting of six boxes with headings taken from the students' book: 'Adjectives', 'Adverbs', 'Similes', 'Metaphor', 'Senses', and 'Feelings'. Each box provides an example for students, e.g. 'tranquil' beach and 'refreshing' water are listed in the 'Adjectives' box. Following the example are two bullet points for students to add their own similes, metaphors etc. about a place that meant a lot to them as a child. When students begin drafting their description they should include their planning work from this sheet.

Year 8 units

Unit 6 Recounts to entertain

Flying Solo

This extract is an informal, entertaining newspaper report. Students will study the following objectives:

◆ Word level: formality and word choice
◆ Sentence level: complex sentences, variety of sentence structure, full range of punctuation, adapting text types, and degrees of formality
◆ Reading: note-making formats, implied and explicit meanings, and development of key ideas
◆ Writing: anticipate reader reaction, effective information, explain complex ideas, and formal description
◆ Speaking and listening: commentary, and listen for a specific purpose.

Going Surfing

Using comic effects in a recount is an important way of entertaining the reader, as this extract shows. These are the objectives students will study:

◆ Word level: formality and word choice, and ironic use of words
◆ Sentence level: variety of sentence structure, adapting text types, and degrees of formality
◆ Reading: implied and explicit meanings, and transposition (how meanings are changed when information is presented in different forms)
◆ Writing: establish the tone, effective information, and formal description.

Planning links

See Unit 6 of *The Literacy Kit Inform, Explain, Describe Overhead Transparencies Pack* for a recount to entertain for whole class work.

Further recount texts are provided throughout the *Inform, Explain, Describe* strand, including simpler and more challenging texts.

Non-fiction to entertain also features in *The Literacy Kit Persuade and Analyse* and *Imagine, Explore, Entertain* strands.

For ready-made lesson starters for all word and sentence level objectives, including those taught in this Unit, see *The Literacy Kit Word* and *Sentence Level Lesson Starters* boxes.

Objectives taught in this unit

Extended writing reinforces objectives taught throughout the unit, plus Speaking and listening 2 Develop recount, and 7 Listen for a specific purpose.

Flying Solo

Word level

12 Formality and word choice (Interpreting the text 9, p. 47; Language and structure 2, 3, p. 47; Writing activity, p. 49)

Sentence level

1 Complex sentences (Language and structure 5, p. 47)

2 Variety of sentence structure (Language and structure 5, p. 47)

3 Full range of punctuation (Language and structure 5, p. 47)

9 Adapting text types (Writing activity, p. 49)

12 Degrees of formality (Interpreting the text 9, p. 47; Language and structure 2, 3, p. 47; Writing activity, p. 49)

Reading

3 Note-making formats (Language and structure 6, p. 48)

7 Implied and explicit meanings (Interpreting the text 10, p. 47)

10 Development of key ideas (Understanding the text 6, p. 46)

Writing

2 Anticipate reader reaction (Writing activity, p. 49)

10 Effective information (Writing activity, p. 49)

11 Explain complex ideas (Writing activity, p. 49)

12 Formal description (Writing activity, p. 49)

Speaking and listening

4 Commentary (Interpreting the text 7, p. 46)

7 Listen for a specific purpose (Interpreting the text 7, p. 46)

Going Surfing

Word level

12 Formality and word choice (Language and structure 5, p. 55)

13 Ironic use of words (Interpreting the text 5, 6, pp. 53–4)

Sentence level

2 Variety of sentence structure (Language and structure 1, 5, pp. 54–5)

9 Adapting text types (Language and structure 5, p. 55)

12 Degrees of formality (Language and structure 5, p. 55)

Reading

7 Implied and explicit meanings (Understanding the text 1–4, p. 53; Interpreting the text 5, p. 53)

8 Transposition (Language and structure 5, p. 55)

Writing

7 Establish the tone (Writing activity, p. 55)

10 Effective information (Writing activity, p. 55)

12 Formal description (Writing activity, p. 55)

Answers

Answers to this unit are provided on page 58 onwards.

Photocopy masters

Photocopy masters for this unit are provided at the back of this book – see Unit 6 PCMs A and B. See also General PCM 6 – Recount.

Notes to photocopy masters

Unit 6 PCM A – Writing a formal newspaper report:1 (Writing activity, p. 49)

This is a framework for students who need a little extra support with the writing activity featured on page 49. Students are provided with a format that progressively takes them through the requirements for producing a formal newspaper report around the crash at Canterbury Airfield. Boxes include topic sentences that the students may or may not wish to use when structuring their own report. Where students wish to produce their own topic sentence, prompts are given to assist with the content and development of the paragraph, and the sequence of the article.

Unit 6 PCM B – Writing a formal newspaper report: 2 (Writing activity, p. 49; Objectives 2, 9, 10, 11, 12)

This is a framework to help students write a formal newspaper report. The opening paragraph prompts them to make reference to the who?, what?, where?, when? and why? of the event being reported. The main focus here is on brevity as each point will be developed as the report progresses. The students are then encouraged, through a series of prompts, to extend the detail of the report. The final section of the framework highlights important points for students to remember when writing their formal newspaper report.

Unit 7 Autobiographical recounts

Healing the Horses

In this extract, the writer gives an account of his own experiences in a form that reads like a novel. Students will learn about the following objectives:

- Word level: unfamiliar words (working out their meaning), and formality and word choice
- Sentence level: adapting text types, and standard English and dialect
- Reading: note-making formats, versatile reading (using a range of reading strategies), and transposition (how meanings are changed when information is presented in different forms)
- Writing: effective planning, effective information, and formal description.

Relative Values

This extract gives a very personal view of a period in the writer's life. These are the objectives students will be studying:

- Word level: prepositions and connectives, and formality and word choice
- Sentence level: variety of sentence structure, colons and semi-colons, grouping sentences, and cohesion and coherence
- Reading: trace developments (of themes and values), and bias and objectivity
- Writing: effective information, and formal description.

Planning links

See Unit 7 of *The Literacy Kit Inform, Explain, Describe Overhead Transparencies Pack* for an autobiographical recount for whole class work.

Further recount texts are provided throughout the *Inform, Explain, Describe* strand, including simpler and more challenging texts.

For ready-made lesson starters for all word and sentence level objectives, including those taught in this Unit, see *The Literacy Kit Word* and *Sentence Level Lesson Starters* boxes.

Objectives taught in this unit

Extended writing reinforces objectives taught throughout the unit, plus Writing 1 Effective planning.

Healing the Horses

Word level

7b Unfamiliar words (Language and structure 1, 3, 4, p. 62)

12 Formality and word choice (Language and structure 1, 3, 4, p. 62)

Sentence level

9 Adapting text types (Writing activity, p. 63)

11 Standard English and dialect (Language and structure 1, 3, 4, p. 62)

Reading

3 Note-making formats (Writing activity, p. 63)

4 Versatile reading (Interpreting the text 7, 8, p. 61)

8 Transposition (Writing activity, p. 63)

Writing

1 Effective planning (Writing activity, p. 63)

10 Effective information (Writing activity, p. 63)

12 Formal description (Writing activity, p. 63)

Relative Values

Word level

10 Prepositions and connectives (Language and structure 2, p. 68)

12 Formality and word choice (Language and structure 1, p. 68)

Sentence level

2 Variety of sentence structure (Language and structure 2, 3, pp. 68–9)

3 Colons and semi-colons (Language and structure 3, p. 69)

6 Grouping sentences (Writing activity, p. 69)

7 Cohesion and coherence (Language and structure 2, p. 68; Writing activity, p. 69)

Reading

5 Trace developments (Interpreting the text 7, p. 67)

6 Bias and objectivity (Interpreting the text 9, 10, p. 67)

Writing

10 Effective information (Writing activity, p. 69)

12 Formal description (Writing activity, p. 69)

Answers

Answers to this unit are provided on page 62 onwards.

Photocopy master

A photocopy master for this unit is provided at the back of this book – see Unit 7 PCM A. See also General PCM 6 – Recount.

Notes to photocopy masters

Unit 7 PCM A – Autobiographical writing (Extended writing, p. 70)

This is a framework to help students structure their own short piece of autobiographical writing. They are encouraged to use either of the brainstorming frames (General PCM 1 or 2) to plan out the content of the writing prior to beginning it. This framework, however, focuses on the use of connectives to help students in the chronological sequencing of their work. Connectives such as *initially*, *in the first place*, *finally* and *eventually* will help students to structure their writing, and to link their sentences and paragraphs. This will make it easier for readers to follow the ideas in the piece of writing.

Unit 8 Information texts

Exploded Drawings

This extract explains some technical information and uses specialist vocabulary. These are the objectives students will be studying:

- ◆ Word level: unfamiliar words (working out their meaning), words in context, specialist vocabulary, and formality and word choice
- ◆ Sentence level: variety of sentence structure, grouping sentences, subject-specific conventions, and degrees of formality
- ◆ Reading: versatile reading (using a range of reading strategies), transposition (how meanings are changed when information is presented in different forms) and development of key ideas
- ◆ Writing: effective information, explain complex ideas, and formal description
- ◆ Speaking and listening: listen for a specific purpose

Planning links

See Unit 8 of *The Literacy Kit Inform, Explain, Describe Overhead Transparencies Pack* for an information text with a technology focus for whole class work.

Further information texts are provided throughout the *Inform, Explain, Describe* strand, including simpler and more challenging texts.

For ready-made lesson starters for all word and sentence level objectives, including those taught in this Unit, see *The Literacy Kit Word* and *Sentence Level Lesson Starters* boxes.

Objectives taught in this unit

Extended writing reinforces objectives taught throughout the unit.

Word level

7b Unfamiliar words (Language and structure 2, p. 76)

7c Words in context (Understanding the text 4, p. 75; Language and structure 2, p. 76)

9 Specialist vocabulary (Language and structure 2, p. 76; Writing activity, p. 77)

12 Formality and word choice (Understanding the text 4, p. 75; Language and structure 2, p. 76)

Sentence level

2 Variety of sentence structure (Language and structure 1, p. 76)

6 Grouping sentences (Interpreting the text 5, 6, p. 75)

8 Subject-specific conventions (Interpreting the text 5, p. 75; Language and structure 2–4, pp. 76–7; Writing activity, p. 77)

12 Degrees of formality (Language and structure 1, 2, p. 76; Language and structure 4, p. 77; Writing activity, p. 77)

Reading

4 Versatile reading (Understanding the text 2, p. 75; Interpreting the text 5, p. 75; Interpreting the text 7, p. 76)

8 Transposition (Language and structure 4, p. 77; Writing activity, p. 77)

10 Development of key ideas (Interpreting the text 5, 6, p. 75)

Writing

10 Effective information (Writing activity, p. 77)

11 Explain complex ideas (Writing activity, p. 77)

12 Formal description (Writing activity, p. 77)

Speaking and listening

7 Listen for a specific purpose (Language and structure 1, p. 76)

Answers

Answers to this unit are provided on page 68 onwards.

Photocopy master

A photocopy master for this unit is provided at the back of this book – see Unit 8 PCM A. See also General PCM 3 – Key words, which supports students in using unfamiliar or technical vocabulary.

Notes to photocopy master

Unit 8 PCM A – Florence Nightingale (Extended writing, p. 78)

This is a worksheet to assist students when organizing the information provided on Florence Nightingale. Each box contains a heading such as 'Significant dates', 'Career details' and 'Interesting historical facts' which will help students to group the facts before starting to write. They are also prompted to consider some of the main conventions of information writing before they produce their information text. They should slowly work their way through the boxes as this will help them to produce an organized piece of writing.

Unit 9 Explanation texts

Why is the sky blue . . . ?

This website page gives an easy-to-follow explanation of what is happening during a process. These are the objectives students will be studying:

◆ Word level: words in context, prepositions and connectives, and formality and word choice
◆ Sentence level: tense shifts, conditionals and modal verbs, subject-specific conventions, and informal to formal (identifying the alterations made to change a text from informal to formal)
◆ Reading: development of key ideas
◆ Writing: effective information

Planning links

See Unit 9 of *The Literacy Kit Inform, Explain, Describe Overhead Transparencies Pack* for explanation texts, with geography and science focuses, for whole class work.

Further explanation texts are provided throughout the *Inform, Explain, Describe* strand, including simpler and more challenging texts.

For ready-made lesson starters for all word and sentence level objectives, including those taught in this Unit, see *The Literacy Kit Word* and *Sentence Level Lesson Starters* boxes.

Objectives taught in this unit

Extended writing reinforces objectives taught throughout the unit, plus Writing 11 Explain complex ideas, and 12 Formal description.

Word level

7c Words in context (Language and structure 5b, p. 83)

10 Prepositions and connectives (Language and structure 6, p. 83)

12 Formality and word choice (Language and structure 5, p. 83)

Sentence level

4 Tense shifts (Language and structure 2, p. 82, Language and structure 3, p. 83)

5 Conditionals and modal verbs (Language and structure 7, p. 84)

8 Subject-specific conventions (Interpreting the text 4, 5, p. 82; Language and structure 6, p. 83; Writing activity, p. 84)

10 Informal to formal (Language and structure 5, p. 83)

Reading

10 Development of key ideas (Language and structure 3, p. 83)

Writing

10 Effective information (Writing activity, p. 84)

Answers

Answers to this unit are provided on page 70 onwards.

Photocopy masters

Photocopy masters for this unit are provided at the back of this book – see Unit 9 PCMs A and B. See also General PCM 7 – Explanation.

Notes to photocopy masters

Unit 9 PCM A – Writing survey: writing for different subjects (Writing activity, p. 84)

This is a worksheet to help students conduct a survey of how writing differs in the different subjects they study in school. Students could either ask other curriculum teachers to fill it in or do it themselves using their own knowledge of each subject's writing demands. The prompts in each box require students to focus on the task and to explain their findings. Ask students to feed back their results and put them into a large display. Discussions could also be organized around the various findings.

Unit 9 PCM B – Writing an explanation (Extended writing, p. 86)

This is a worksheet to support students in writing their own explanation text. It flags to students the key stylistic conventions they should remember, and can also be used as a planning and drafting frame.

Year 9 units

Unit 10 Media recounts

An Ealing Comedy of Errors

This extract gives newspaper readers the facts about a news event. These are the objectives students will be studying:

◆ Word level: layers of meaning
◆ Sentence level: degrees of formality, integrate speech, reference and quotation, and paragraph organization
◆ Reading: evaluate information, readers and texts (how they influence each other), author's standpoint, and rhetorical devices
◆ Writing: 'infotainment' (how information texts can be amusing and entertaining), and descriptive detail.

The Lancashire Cat Mystery

This extract treats an unusual event in an original way. Students will be studying these objectives:

◆ Word level: connectives for developing thought
◆ Sentence level: degrees of formality, integrate speech, reference and quotation, and paragraph organization
◆ Reading: evaluate information, readers and texts (how they influence each other), author's standpoint, and rhetorical devices
◆ Writing: creativity in non-literary texts, 'infotainment' (how information texts can be amusing and entertaining), and descriptive detail.

Planning links

See Unit 10 of *The Literacy Kit Inform, Explain, Describe Overhead Transparencies Pack* for a media recount for whole class work.

Further recount texts are provided throughout the *Inform, Explain, Describe* strand, including simpler texts.

For ready-made lesson starters for all word and sentence level objectives, including those taught in this Unit, see *The Literacy Kit Word* and *Sentence Level Lesson Starters* boxes.

Objectives taught in this unit

Extended writing reinforces objectives taught throughout the unit, plus Writing 4 Presentational devices, and 12 Effective presentation of information.

An Ealing Comedy of Errors

Word level

7 Layers of meaning (Interpreting the text 5, p. 91; Interpreting the text 7–9, p. 92)

Sentence level

3 Degrees of formality (Language and structure 2b, 3, pp. 92–3)

4 Integrate speech, reference and quotation (Language and structure 2a, p. 92, Writing activity, p. 93)

6 Paragraph organization (Language and structure 1, p. 92)

Reading

4 Evaluate information (Interpreting the text 6–9, pp. 91–2)

8 Readers and texts (Interpreting the text 5–9, pp. 91–2)

11 Author's standpoint (Interpreting the text 5–9, pp. 91–2)

12 Rhetorical devices (Interpreting the text 5–9, pp. 91–2; Language and structure 1, p. 92)

Writing

7 'Infotainment' (Interpreting the text 5–9, pp. 91–2; Language and structure 1, 2, p. 92; Writing activity, p. 93)

11 Descriptive detail (Language and structure 2, p. 92; Writing activity, p. 93)

The Lancashire Cat Mystery

Word level

8 Connectives for developing thought (Language and structure 3, p. 97)

Sentence level

3 Degrees of formality (Language and structure 2, p. 97)

4 Integrate speech, reference and quotation (Interpreting the text 10, p. 96; Writing activity, p. 97)

6 Paragraph organization (Interpreting the text 8, 10, p. 96; Language and structure 1, 3, p. 97; Writing activity, p. 97)

Reading

4 Evaluate information (Interpreting the text 6, 9, p. 96)

8 Readers and texts (Interpreting the text 6–10, p. 96; Language and structure 1, p. 97)

11 Author's standpoint (Interpreting the text 6, 9, p. 96)

12 Rhetorical devices (Interpreting the text 6–10, p. 96; Language and structure 1, p. 97)

Writing

6 Creativity in non-literary texts (Interpreting the text 10, p. 96; Writing activity, p. 97)

7 'Infotainment' (Interpreting the text 10, p. 96; Writing activity, p. 97)

11 Descriptive detail (Writing activity, p. 97)

Answers

Answers to this unit are provided on page 73 onwards.

Photocopy master

A photocopy master for this unit is provided at the back of this book – see Unit 10 PCM A. See also General PCM 6 – Recount.

Notes to photocopy master

Unit 10 PCM A – Writing an informal newspaper report (Extended writing, p. 98)

This is a frame to assist students in the extended writing activity where they are asked to create a recount about a crime for a national newspaper. Starter lines are included as prompts for students to include quotations, and also to structure the article so that it retells the events of the night.

Unit 11 Travel writing

Sinking Fast

This extract is a very dramatic and entertaining recount of an incident that took place on a journey. Students will be studying the following objectives:

♦ Word level: terminology for analysis (using appropriate terms for analysing language), and layers of meaning
♦ Sentence level: complex sentences, and punctuation for clarity and effect
♦ Reading: rhetorical devices
♦ Writing: 'infotainment' (how information texts can be amusing and entertaining), integrate information, and descriptive detail.

A Desert Dies

This extract gives a highly descriptive recount of the traveller's experiences. These are the objectives students will study:

♦ Word level: layers of meaning
♦ Sentence level: degrees of formality
♦ Reading: note-making at speed, and rhetorical devices
♦ Writing: creativity in non-literary texts, and integrate information.

Planning links

See Unit 11 of *The Literacy Kit Inform, Explain, Describe Overhead Transparencies Pack* for a dramatic recount (travel writing) for whole class work.

Further recount texts are provided throughout the *Inform, Explain, Describe* strand, including simpler texts.

For ready-made lesson starters for all word and sentence level objectives, including those taught in this Unit, see *The Literacy Kit Word* and *Sentence Level Lesson Starters* boxes.

Objectives taught in this unit

Extended writing reinforces objectives taught throughout the unit, plus Writing 11 Descriptive detail.

Sinking Fast

Word level

6 Terminology for analysis (Interpreting the text 6, p. 102; Language and structure 3, p. 103)

7 Layers of meaning (Interpreting the text 4, 6, p. 102; Language and structure 3, p. 103)

Sentence level

1 Complex sentences (Interpreting the text 5b, p. 102; Language and structure 2b, p. 103, Writing activity, p. 104)

2 Punctuation for clarity and effect (Language and structure 1, p. 103; Writing activity, p. 104)

Reading

12 Rhetorical devices (Interpreting the text 4–6, p. 102; Language and structure 1–3, p. 103)

Writing

7 'Infotainment' (Interpreting the text 4–6, p. 102; Language and structure 1–3, p. 103; Writing activity, p. 104)

9 Integrate information (Writing activity, p. 104)

11 Descriptive detail (Writing activity, p. 104)

A Desert Dies

Word level

7 Layers of meaning (Language and structure 1, 2, p. 108)

Sentence level

3 Degrees of formality (Writing activity, p. 109)

Reading

3 Note-making at speed (Writing activity, p. 109)

12 Rhetorical devices (Language and structure 1–4, p. 108)

Writing

6 Creativity in non-literary texts (Language and structure 1, 3–4, p. 108)

9 Integrate information (Writing activity, p. 109)

Answers

Answers to this unit are provided on page 77 onwards.

Photocopy master

A photocopy master for this unit is provided at the back of this book – see Unit 11 PCM A.

Notes to photocopy master

Unit 11 PCM A – Describing a journey (Extended writing, p. 110)

This is a frame to assist students in the extended writing activity where they are asked to retell a journey with vivid description. The frame provides prompts and examples for students to follow when completing each section of the description, such as using active verbs, third person, and similes or metaphors.

Unit 12 Information texts to persuade

Choosing to Be Vegetarian

Here we compare two examples of information texts that intend to persuade their audience to do something: a leaflet and a web page. Students will be studying the following objectives:

- Word level: apply knowledge (of word origins), and connectives for developing thought
- Sentence level: paragraph organization, and conventions of ICT texts
- Reading: synthesize information (put it together from different sources), evaluate information, compare texts, and author's standpoint

- Writing: presentational devices, integrate information, explain connections, and effective presentation of information.

Planning links

See Unit 12 of *The Literacy Kit Inform, Explain, Describe Overhead Transparencies Pack* for an information text, that also persuades/instructs, for whole class work.

Further information texts are provided throughout the *Inform, Explain, Describe* strand, including simpler texts.

For a full range of persuasive texts, see *The Literacy Kit Persuade and Analyse* strand.

For ready-made lesson starters for all word and sentence level objectives, including those taught in this Unit, see *The Literacy Kit Word* and *Sentence Level Lesson Starters* boxes.

Objectives taught in this unit

Extended writing reinforces objectives taught throughout the unit.

Word level

4b Apply knowledge (Language and structure 2, p. 118)

8 Connectives for developing thought (Language and structure 4, p. 119)

Sentence level

6 Paragraph organization (Language and structure 4, p. 119)

8 Conventions of ICT texts (Language and structure 4, p. 119)

Reading

2 Synthesize information (Writing activity, p. 119)

4 Evaluate information (Interpreting the text 11, p. 117, Language and structure 3, p. 119)

7 Compare texts (Interpreting the text 12, p. 118)

11 Author's standpoint (Interpreting the text 9–11, p. 117; Language and structure 3, p. 119)

Writing

4 Presentational devices (Interpreting the text 9, 10, p. 117; Writing activity, p. 119)

9 Integrate information (Writing activity, p. 119)

10 Explain connections (Writing activity, p. 119)

12 Effective presentation of information (Writing activity, p. 119)

Speaking and listening

1 Evaluate own talk (Speaking and listening, pp. 121–2)

2 Standard English (Speaking and listening, pp. 121–2)

5 Compare points of view (Speaking and listening, pp. 121–2)

6 Analyse bias (Speaking and listening, pp. 121–2)

7 Identify underlying issues (Speaking and listening, pp. 121–2)

8 Evaluate own contributions (Speaking and listening, pp. 121–2)

9 Considered viewpoint (Speaking and listening, pp. 121–2)

10 Group organization (Speaking and listening, pp. 121–2)

Answers

Answers to this unit are provided on page 82 onwards.

Photocopy master

A photocopy master for this unit is provided at the back of this book – see Unit 12 PCM A. See also General PCM 2 – Brainstorming, for arguments.

Notes to photocopy master

Unit 12 PCM A – Writing a leaflet (Extended writing, p. 120)

This is a frame to assist students in the extended writing activity where they are asked to write an information leaflet on 'Why you might want to cut down on eating meat'. The frame provides a structure for students to use when selecting appropriate information for the purpose and audience, and includes bullet point prompts such as 'A healthy diet consists of:' and 'Reasons for cutting down on eating meat'.

Unit 13 Explanations

Tollund Man

This extract explains the results of a scientific investigation. These are the objectives students will be studying:

- ◆ Word level: connectives for developing thought
- ◆ Sentence level: degrees of formality, paragraph organization, and sustained standard English
- ◆ Reading: information retrieval
- ◆ Writing: review own writing, exploratory writing, formal essay, narrative techniques, and explain connections.

Planning links

See Unit 13 of *The Literacy Kit Inform, Explain, Describe Overhead Transparencies Pack* for an explanation text with a different curriculum focus (features of literary texts) for whole class work.

Further explanation texts are provided throughout the *Inform, Explain, Describe* strand, including simpler texts.

For ready-made lesson starters for all word and sentence level objectives, including those taught in this Unit, see *The Literacy Kit Word* and *Sentence Level Lesson Starters* boxes.

Objectives taught in this unit

Extended writing reinforces objectives taught throughout the unit, plus Sentence level 5 Shape paragraphs rapidly.

Word level

8 Connectives for developing thought (Language and structure 5, p. 127)

Sentence level

3 Degrees of formality (Language and structure 2, p. 126)

6 Paragraph organization (Language and structure 4, p. 127; Writing activity, p. 128)

9 Sustained standard English (Writing activity, p. 128)

Reading

1 Information retrieval (Understanding the text 1–5, p. 126; Interpreting the text, 6–8, p. 126)

Writing

1 Review own writing (Writing activity, p. 128)

2 Exploratory writing (Writing activity, p. 128)

3 Formal essay (Writing activity, p. 128)

5 Narrative techniques (Writing activity, p. 128)

10 Explain connections (Writing activity, p. 128)

Answers

Answers to this unit are provided on page 86 onwards.

Photocopy masters

Photocopy masters for this unit are provided at the back of this book – see Unit 13 PCMs A and B. See also General PCMs 7 – Explanation and 8 – Types of writing used in subjects.

Notes to photocopy masters

Unit 13 PCMs A and B – Tollund Man History/English assignment (Writing activity, p. 128)

These are frames to assist students in the writing activity where they are asked to write different assignments on Tollund Man, according to the requirements of History and English lessons. The frames provide a structure for students to follow, giving prompts for the type of response required. For example, the History assignment focuses on factual responses, such as details about the usefulness of Tollund Man to scientists. The English assignment focuses more on imaginative, descriptive ideas such as describing the faces of the scientists with similes or metaphors.

Unit 14 Playing with non-fiction conventions

The Glamis Herald

This extract takes the events of a Shakespeare play (*Macbeth*) and creates a parody of a newspaper report about politicians. Students will be studying these objectives:

- Word level: layers of meaning
- Sentence level: exploit conventions
- Reading: readers and texts (how they influence each other), and author's standpoint
- Writing: 'infotainment' (how information texts can be amusing and entertaining), and descriptive detail.

Planning links

See Unit 14 of *The Literacy Kit Inform, Explain, Describe Overhead Transparencies Pack* for snippets of a range of non-fiction text types that could be used to revise stylistic conventions of non-fiction during whole class work prior to attempting a parody.

Further examples of non-fiction texts are provided throughout *The Literacy Kit*.

For ready-made lesson starters for all word and sentence level objectives, including those taught in this Unit, see *The Literacy Kit Word* and *Sentence Level Lesson Starters* boxes.

Objectives taught in this unit

Extended writing reinforces objectives taught throughout the unit, plus Writing 1 Review own writing.

Word level

7 Layers of meaning (Interpreting the text 5, 6, p. 134; Interpreting the text 8, p. 135; Language and structure 4, p. 136)

Sentence level

7 Exploit conventions (Interpreting the text 5, p. 134; Language and structure 4, p. 136; Writing activity, p. 136)

Reading

8 Readers and texts (Interpreting the text 5, p. 134; Interpreting the text 8, p. 135)

11 Author's standpoint (Interpreting the text 6, p. 134; Interpreting the text 8, p. 135)

Writing

7 'Infotainment' (Interpreting the text 5, 8, pp. 134–5; Language and structure 4, p. 136; Writing activity, p. 136)

11 Descriptive detail (Language and structure 2, p. 135)

Answers

Answers to this unit are provided on page 87 onwards.

Photocopy master

A photocopy master for this unit is provided at the back of this book – see Unit 14 PCM A. See also General PCM 9 – Conventions of different types of writing.

Notes to photocopy master

Unit 14 PCM A – Writing a parody: estate agent's report (Extended writing, p. 138)

This is a frame to assist students in writing a parody of a non-fiction text type – in this case, estate agent reports. An example is provided of one based on Macbeth. The conventions of an estate agent report are included, such as use of an impersonal voice, and an often informal and exaggerated style. Students should use a text of their choice, perhaps a class reader, as the resource for their own parody of an estate agent report.

A further note on planning links

Inform, Explain, Describe Overhead Transparencies Pack contains three further texts to help you meet objectives for this strand. 'Stylistic conventions of email', and 'Publisher's web page' address ICT text requirements; 'Standard English and dialectal variation' gives a focused look at a piece of dialect, including non-standard English grammar and spelling.

Notes to the general photocopy masters

The general photocopy masters on pages at the back of this book (see General PCMs 1–11) may be used in any year, depending on the level of support or practice needed by students. Teachers may wish to photocopy these sheets onto acetate and use them to model key skills in a whole-class teaching session.

General PCM 1 – Brainstorming

This is a frame to help students collect and structure their ideas around a topic. It may be used in preparation for creative writing, for structuring an information text, or for structuring information for an explanation text. It can also be used to secure students' use of paragraphing.

General PCM 2 – Brainstorming for arguments

This is a frame to help students collect and structure their ideas around a topic, looking at ideas for and against a point under discussion. The boxes also prompt students to find evidence to support the points they are raising, and the space at the bottom encourages students to reach a conclusion about their argument.

General PCM 3 – Key words

This is a sheet to help students keep a record of key words, including the meaning/ function of the word and an example of it in context. This should be an individual record which students complete independently according to need, though occasionally it may be appropriate for a whole class to enter a new key word simultaneously. This sheet could also be used across the curriculum.

General PCM 4 – Research grid

This is a chart to assist students when they are researching a topic. For example, if students are researching a famous person they would write the person's name for the main heading and list some general facts about them, e.g. age, occupation. Students should then decide on the areas they would like to research in more detail, e.g. hobbies, family, likes, dislikes; these then become the subheadings. Students can then list three pieces of information as bullet points in note form under each of the subheadings. If students later need to present their findings, either written or orally, this frame will help them to structure their paragraphs/points.

General PCM 5 – Information

This frame can be used to investigate the different forms of information text. It can act as a reminder to students of the best text to turn to when they are researching information. It can also be used as a prompt in considering audience and purpose when composing their own information texts.

General PCM 6 – Recount

This frame supports students in analysing recount texts. The top section can be used when studying a text to discover which of the features of recount writing it displays. The lower section can be used to check students' understanding of the features of recount writing, and can be revisited as a prompt when writing recounts.

General PCM 7 – Explanation

Some of the key features of explanation texts are listed in question form in the first column of this copymaster. The aim is to support students in analysing the effectiveness of explanation texts. The second column provides a check of understanding by asking students to quote examples – this is also a useful exercise to encourage close reference to, and quotation from, the text. The sheet can also be used to review students' own writing of explanation texts. By noting in the third column those features that they have not deployed, students will be prompted to redraft those areas in which their text is weakest.

General PCM 8 – Types of writing used in subjects

This frame encourages students to apply their learning about non-fiction text types to their work across the curriculum. Liaise with subject heads to teach the application of non-fiction forms in their work. The sheet can be filled out for a range of different text types, and then used as prompt for writing in the future.

General PCM 9 – Conventions of different types of writing

This is a simple 'reminder sheet' of the features of text types. After learning about each text type, students can complete one part of the sheet, filling in the text type and its key features. The sheet can then be used as a simple revision aid, or as a prompt to check for appropriateness of style and structure in writing tasks in English and across the curriculum.

General PCM 10 – Instruction texts

This is a frame that offers a general structure for writing instruction texts. There are four boxes headed 'Purpose', 'Equipment', 'Instructions' and 'Final tips' which will help students organize their writing appropriately. The box headed 'Instructions' offers students sentence starters, e.g. *First* and *Finally*, to help them sequence their instructions logically.

General PCM 11 – Speaking and listening

This is a frame to help students structure their ideas around a persuasive speech, which may be used as part of an explain or inform project. The different sections and prompts help students to order their facts and arguments, allowing for an opening statement, development of the main point, a recognition of opposing views followed by counter arguments, and a conclusion.

Answers

Year 7 units

Unit 1 Information texts
Formal writing: Young Citizen's Passport

Understanding the text

1 What kind of work may children under the age of 14 legally do?

Occasional light farm work (supervised by a parent); parts in plays or films (with a licence from the local authority)

2 Is the age for starting work the same in all areas?

No, it varies according to the type of work and local authority rules.

3 How long may a child under 16 work before the start of the school day?

No more than one hour

4 In what kind of bar may people under 18 work?

One in a restaurant serving drinks with meals

An above average answer will add that under-18s can also work in other kinds of bar as part of a Modern Apprenticeship for the licensing trade.

Interpreting the text

5 An information text for young people should look lively and attractive. Look at the layout of the page. How has the designer tried to do this here? Say something about:
- the images

   They are bold, brightly coloured, and in a technical style.
- the use of boxes and panels around text

   Panels are used to make headings stand out. The feature on employment rights and the story of the boy who was injured at work are boxed to set them apart.
- the choice of font styles.

   The fonts are very clear and easy to read.

6 Look at the first paragraph – what is the source of the facts about what the law says? How much can you 'trust' in what you have learned from this text? Does giving the source make the text feel reliable and factual? Write a brief paragraph explaining your response.

The information derives from the Children and Young Persons Act 1933. Giving this source at the beginning of the text adds authority to the information, as it is clearly taken from an official source.

Language and structure

1 Information texts can be written in the third person, like this:

No young person below school leaving age may be employed . . .

They can also be written in the second person, like this:

If you are below school leaving age, you may not be employed . . .

Choose one paragraph and rewrite it using the second-person form. Does this make it sound more personal? Write a sentence saying whether you think the text becomes more or less easy to follow as a result.

Possible rewrites:

- *The only employment you can be given if you are under 14 is . . .*
- *If you are aged 14 or over, you may only be employed in light work approved by your local authority.*
- *If you are below school leaving age, you cannot be employed before 7am or after 7pm, for more . . .*
- *New rules require you to have a magistrates' licence to be paid to take part in a sport if you are between 14 and 16.*

Whether this sounds more personal or is easier to follow is a matter of personal opinion. More able students may notice that the use of 'you' alone does not greatly affect how personal the text feels, as it is still in a very formal style. It is not likely to make much difference to how easy the text is to follow.

2 Information texts are usually written in the present tense. Find an example in this text of a sentence in the past tense. Say why this change of tense is necessary.

Examples include:

- *A boy of 14, working in a factory making beds, suffered severe injuries when his arm was trapped in an unguarded machine.*
- *A court fined his employer £1000 for failing to fit a guard to the machine and £200 for employing a child.*
- *The employer also paid £438 towards the cost of the case.*

The sentences are in the past tense because they describe individual events which have happened, rather than describing the general situation as it is now.

3 Information texts need to be clearly organized. How are different points linked together in this text? Write down three words or phrases which the writer uses to link ideas.

Linking words:

- *these*
- *although*
- *or*
- *however*
- *unless*
- *as a result*
- *even if.*

4 The writer of an information text often makes some general points and then backs them up with specific examples.

Use a table like this to show two examples of the way this writer supports ideas with examples. Fill in the missing information.

General point	Supporting example(s)
Only certain kinds of work are available for children under 14	*Occasional light farm work; parts in plays or films*
There are few restrictions on the employment of 16 or 17 year olds	People under 18 cannot normally work in a bar

Informal writing: A Guide to Health

Understanding the text

1 What are the four main types of foods?

Types of foods:

- *carbohydrates*
- *dairy*
- *meat, fish, protein*
- *fruit and vegetables.*

2 Write down one tip that the writer gives for creating a balanced diet.

Any of the following:

- *eat 5–9 servings of carbohydrates a day*
- *eat 5–9 servings of fruit and vegetables a day*
- *eat 2–3 servings of dairy foods a day*
- *eat low fat meat, fish or protein*
- *eat 2–3 servings of meat, fish or protein a day*
- *use fatty, sugary foods sparingly.*

3 How much food does the average person eat in a lifetime?

100 tonnes

4 What are micronutrients?

Vitamins and minerals

Interpreting the text

5 If you had to pick out the three main ideas in the text, what would they be?

Main ideas:

- *food is important for health*
- *there are four different types of food*
- *a balanced diet is eating the right amount of each type of food.*

6 Information needs to be presented clearly. Nick Vollmer uses some diagrams (e.g. the pyramid) and some images (e.g. clip-art showing a pig on a bike). Which of his presentational devices do you think work best? Which would you have done differently?

Personal opinion. Answers might comment on the quality and relevance of illustration. More advanced answers should note that the pie chart and pyramid diagram would be clearer and more useful if they were placed beside the text rather than behind it. This would also make the text easier to read.

7 The leaflet is aimed at students aged 11–14. How might the text have been different if it was aimed at:

a an older audience (e.g. aged 35–50)

There could be:

- *more text*
- *longer sentences*
- *less illustration*
- *different style of illustration*
- *more adult type style.*

b a younger audience (9–11)?

There could be:

- *more pictures*
- *less text*
- *shorter sentences*
- *more information put across by pictures instead of text.*

Language and structure

1 Look at the way the writer organizes his information. Compare the information he puts on each side of his leaflet by completing these sentences:

    a The first side of the leaflet gives information on . . .

    food facts in general.

    b The second side of the leaflet gives information on . . .

    health in general, and more detail of what you should eat to be healthy.

2 The writer uses a variety of sentence functions in the leaflet. Find an example of:

- a statement

  Possible answers (there are others in the text):

  25–30% of the food we eat should be fats

  In your lifetime, you eat 100 tonnes of food

  You can be physically or mentally unhealthy

  Dairy foods are any foods or drink containing milk or butter

- a question

  How much should we be eating?

- a command.

  One of the following:

  Try to get 2–3 servings of dairy foods a day

  Use fatty, sugary foods sparingly

  Use a variety of foods

3 Nick Vollmer is writing for an audience aged 11–14. A good information text will use language to appeal to its age group. Find examples where Nick:

- uses headings to grab the reader's interest

  The statistics; Fun Facts; All Health; Types of Food; A balanced Diet

- addresses the reader directly.

You can be physically or mentally unhealthy

This will help you to understand . . .

You should get 5–9 servings of carbs. a day

4 Information texts can include commands that directly address the reader. Look at the tone this writer uses when he gives commands. He could have said: 'Eat 2–3 servings of dairy foods a day'. This would sound impersonal and more like an order. How does he make his commands seem more personal and friendly?

He says 'you should' or 'try to' rather than phrasing his commands as orders.

5 Nick Vollmer's leaflet contains a number of spelling or typing errors. He uses a personal spelling notebook at school. Which words do you notice that he should add to his book and learn to spell accurately?

Possible answers (there are others in the text):

- *'in you're lifetime' should be 'your'*
- *'vitimins' should be 'vitamins'*

- *'e.i.' should be 'e.g.'*
- *'catagories' should be 'categories'*
- *'regoin' should be 'region'.*

6 Imagine you are Nick Vollmer's teacher and you are marking his leaflet. What feedback would you give him? What do you think are its strengths and weaknesses?

Writing as if you are his teacher, give him three brief comments on:

a the presentation of his leaflet

b the way he uses language

c suggestions of ways to improve it.

You could also give him a grade or mark out of ten.

Personal opinion. Here is a possible answer:

a *The presentation is good and looks lively. Use of bullet points helps to make it clear.*

b *The sentences are short, keeping the message clear for a young age group.*

c *The illustrations and diagrams could be placed beside the text instead of behind it for greater clarity. The 'All Health' section could be better linked to the rest of the leaflet; it seems like a separate topic.*

Unit 2 Recounts
Autobiographical writing: Millvina Dean, Survivor of the Titanic

Understanding the text

1 How many Titanic survivors were left at the time Millvina Dean gave her interview?

Five

2 How old was she when the ship sank?

Nine weeks old

3 How many members of her family were on the Titanic and how many survived?

Four; three survived (her mother, brother and herself survived; her father died)

4 How is Millvina Dean still involved with the Titanic?

She goes to Titanic conventions and exhibitions and other Titanic-related events, as a guest.

5 Why does she not wish to watch the film *Titanic*?

She thinks it will upset her by making her think about how her father died.

6 Summarize what you think are the three main points made in the text.

Possible answer:

- *she's the youngest survivor of the Titanic*
- *her father was lost with the ship*
- *she has travelled the world because of her connections with the Titanic.*

Interpreting the text

7 How reliable do you find Millvina Dean's account? Does her recount feel like a historical document, full of accurate facts? Say why or why not.

The recount is not like a historical document because it is more about Millvina Dean's feelings than facts. There are some facts about steerage class and specific lifeboats, but the recount is mostly about her life as an adult and her involvement in the Titanic industry.

8   Write down one thing you learn about Millvina Dean's character from the text.

Possible answers:

- *she is fond of her family*
- *she feels proud of her father's quick reaction and how it saved them*
- *she likes to remember her father even though he died when she was tiny*
- *she enjoys the celebrity and being fussed over.*

9   What is Millvina Dean's attitude to the celebrity status (fame) she has achieved? Do you think she welcomes the attention or does she try to avoid it? Write a short paragraph saying how you can tell.

She clearly enjoys the celebrity status; nothing suggests she tries to avoid it.

Evidence to back this up:

- *she says, 'people make a terrific fuss of me, which I like!'*
- *her words, 'I've been on several cruises and even given a talk on the QE2,' suggest she is living the high life*
- *she does not complain about the number of letters she receives*
- *she seems quite proud of the amount of travelling she does, the receptions held for her and the road named after her.*

Language and structure

1   Look at the first sentence of the article.

   a   Why do you think the writer chose this as the first sentence?

      It links directly to the Titanic and feels quite personal.

   b   Do you think it is a good beginning for the article?

      Personal opinion. It is a more original and gripping opening than starting with the name, age, etc. of Millvina Dean.

2   Look at the end of the first sentence, where the writer uses the phrase 'you see'. Does this phrase make the text seem . . .

more chatty – more formal – more informal – too relaxed – friendly – like a letter

Choose the best description. Then write a sentence explaining your choice.

Various options can be justified:

More chatty: it sounds conversational, as though you are talking with Millvina.

More formal: no evidence for this.

More informal: the conversational tone sounds informal and appealing.

Too relaxed: possibly; it does sound very informal, but this seems appropriate to the subject-matter and the publication.

Friendly: it gives an instant feeling of being with Millvina, talking to her, so it feels direct and personal.

Like a letter: no; this is not a phrase specifically used in letters.

3   Recounts can use a wide range of sentences. Most of Millvina Dean's sentences are complex, e.g. 'We travelled steerage – that's third class – and most of the third-class passengers were to die because they couldn't get from the lower decks to the lifeboats.'

A few sentences are simple, e.g. 'They were exactly like him.'

Which of these statements do you think best describes the effect of this range of sentences? Choose the opening of the statement you most agree with, and then finish it off in your own words.

   a   The variety of sentences makes the text vivid because . . .

b   The variety of sentences makes the text hard to follow because . . .

c   The variety of sentences holds our interest because . . .

d   The variety of sentences makes the text feel like a spoken account because . . .

Any of the sentence beginnings could be chosen, although the most appropriate answer is d. The variety of sentences makes the text feel like a spoken account because it sounds as if it has not been prepared and thought through in advance.

4   How does the writer link the different ideas in the text together? Look for three words or phrases which help to do this.

Possible answers:

- *but*
- *until*
- *because*
- *since then*
- *now.*

5   Recounts are usually written in the past tense. Here, the writer describes the events of the Titanic using the past tense, and writes about her life now using the present tense. Find sentences which illustrate both tenses.

Past tense:

Any sentence about the past, e.g. 'Until the wreck was discovered there wasn't nearly so much interest in the disaster.'

Present tense:

Any sentence about her life now, e.g. 'I can't bear ice in my drinks – it always makes me think of the iceberg, you see.'

6   Although Millvina Dean's recount is not all in chronological order, some paragraphs *do* tell events in the order they happened. Which paragraphs do this?

Paragraphs 3 and 4, which tell the story of the Titanic sinking and her life since then

7   At the end of the text it says 'Millvina Dean was talking to David Gillard'. In other words, the article is based on an interview. Yet it is written as if it were a personal account. Does this change your view on how valid or reliable the text is?

Write a sentence or two describing how you think the text has been written, and by whom.

Most students should recognize that the text was written by David Gillard, but heavily based on an interview with Millvina Dean. More advanced answers will show awareness that the writer has selected which parts of the interview to use, so the personal nature of the account is not as reliable as it might seem. Even so, everything in the piece should have come from the interview.

8   Using the article you have read, complete this fact file about Millvina Dean:

Name: *Millvina Dean*

Age: 88

Where she lives: *Southampton / New Forest*

What she now does: *retired / travels to speak at Titanic conventions*

What she did earlier in her life: *cartographer, secretary, assistant in tobacconist's shop*

What happened to her father: *he went down with the Titanic, after making sure his wife and children escaped*

What happened to her mother, her brother and herself on the Titanic: *they were sent up to the lifeboats by her father as soon as they heard the sound of the crash. She was bundled in a sack and thrown into lifeboat 13; her mother was in the same lifeboat. They were reunited with her brother (who was in a different lifeboat) when they were picked up by the Carpathia.*

How the Titanic disaster has affected her life positively and negatively:

negatively – she grew up without a father

positively – she has become a celebrity through her connection with the disaster

What kind of person she is: *fond of her family; sentimental; greatly enjoying her celebrity status*

Personal recounts: My First Day at School

Understanding the text

1 Make a set of notes which show clearly:

- the name of each speaker
- what the speaker is best known for
- two or three main points of what they remember about the first day at school.

Here are some sample answers; others are possible.

Name	Best known as	Main points
Glenys Kinnock	MEP	Went to grandmother's first, not nervous Teacher was friendly Sweet at end of day
Benjamin Zephaniah	Poet	Went with sister, who cried all day Enjoyed it, playing all day Hated school later and sister liked it
Esther Rantzen	Chairman of ChildLine	Started at two-and-three-quarters Very miserable, painted black paintings Thought it was pointless, but liked school later
Brian Keenan	Novelist, former Beirut hostage	Remembers only first day at secondary school, not primary Went on bus – first time without parents Everyone looked different in school uniform

2   Glenys Kinnock has vivid memories of a teacher. Summarize the information we learn about this teacher.
Her name was Miss Morgan Jones. She was 'very large, very cuddly and very nice.' She gave out sweets to good children at the end of the school day, and was very kind: most children got a sweet.

Interpreting the text

3   Which speaker do you think has the most positive memory of the first day at school? How can you tell?
Glenys Kinnock: she has nothing negative to say about the school or any aspect of the experience, unlike the other writers. (Brian Keenan is neutral but even he remembers that 'everyone was apprehensive'; Benjamin Zephaniah mentions disowning his sister and hating school later.)

4   Which speaker has the least positive memory? Again, how can you tell?
Esther Rantzen: from the beginning, she uses words like 'traumatic' and 'miserable'. Although she says she enjoyed school later, most of her piece is about how much she disliked school at first and why she thinks she was too young to be sent there.

5   Which speaker's experience of school sounds most *different* from the kind of school you first attended? Think about activities you did at school and the teachers you have known. Do they remind you of the experiences described by the writers? Write a brief paragraph to explain your answer.
An acceptable answer will be written in complete sentences and compare own experiences with the writers'. A more developed answer might give reasons why the experiences might be so different.

Language and structure

1   Recounts are usually divided into paragraphs about different parts of the subject. They may use complex sentences with subordinate clauses, where information is packed together densely.
Choose either the Glenys Kinnock text or the Benjamin Zephaniah text. Then:
   a   write a very brief summary of what each paragraph is about (ideally try to use just one word – e.g. 'teacher', 'classroom', 'sister')
   b   write a sentence saying why the paragraphs are in this order – would they make sense in a different one?
   c   choose one paragraph and say how its opening sentence helps prepare the reader for some new information
   d   choose a complex sentence and say whether it is easy to follow or not.
   Glenys Kinnock
   a   *Grandmother's house / before school; teacher and classroom; sweets*
   b   *Chronological order through the day; they only really make sense in this order*
   c   *Paragraph 1: suggests what will follow – that she was not nervous*
   Paragraph 2: describing the teacher introduces the friendly atmosphere of the school
   d   *Complex sentences are all easy to follow.*
   Benjamin Zephaniah
   a   *Sister crying; playing in school; disowning sister; changes as they grew up*
   b   *Chronological order from arriving at school to later reactions to school; they only really make sense in this order*
   c   *Paragraph 1: introduces the fact that it will be about himself and his sister*
   Paragraph 2: introduces his reaction to school
   Paragraph 3: moves the focus back to his relationship with his sister
   Paragraph 4: moves the focus on to later reactions to school

d   *Complex sentences are all easy to follow.*

2   Choose either the Esther Rantzen or the Brian Keenan text. Look at whether the writer uses the past tense, the present tense, or both. Write down which it is, then give a reason why the writer may have used tenses in this way.

Esther Rantzen

Past and present: past to describe her first day at school and what she did with her own children; present to talk about her current feelings about schooling

Brian Keenan

Past and present: past to describe memories of school and trying to recall memories when in captivity; present to say 'I remember', describing what he now recalls.

Unit 3 Explanation texts
Formal and informal writing: Mobile Phones

Understanding the texts

Text A

1   What two reasons does the leaflet give for young people using mobile phones?
Personal security; keeping in touch with others

2   Does it state that mobile phones carry a health risk?
No, but it does say they affect brain activity.

3   What are the findings of the expert group?
That if there were health risks, children and young people would be more at risk than adults because their heads and nervous systems are still developing

4   What are UK CMOs?
Chief Medical Officers for the UK

5   What advice does the leaflet give young people about using mobile phones?
Use them only for essential purposes; keep all calls short

Text B

6   What is the difference between adult and child skulls?
Child skulls are thinner than adult ones.

7   Does the website say that there are definite dangers in using mobile phones when you are young?
No, but there is a possibility of some risk.

8   What is the advice about mobile phone masts at schools?
That they should not be placed there

Both texts

9   When you were answering questions 1–8, which features of each text helped you to find the information you needed? Name one key feature of each text. You might mention something specific about:
   ●   layout
   ●   the way the information is structured
   ●   the use of language.
Personal opinion.

Text A might be seen as harder to navigate: long paragraphs and sentences, and quite complex language;

bullet points should have helped with question 5.

Information in Text B might be considered to be more accessible: layout divides information into short sections; bold type makes information stand out; language is simpler.

Interpreting the text

10 In what ways is the information in the two texts similar?

Both texts:

- *report government research about mobile phones*
- *say that children should be more careful about how they use them*
- *say there is no proven health risk*
- *say that if a health risk existed, children would be in more danger than adults*
- *say that children's bodies are still developing*
- *say that calls should be kept as short as possible.*

11 In what ways does the information differ?

Text A:

- *says that mobile phones affect brain activity*
- *says there is a lot we don't yet know*
- *defines children as under 16*
- *says the UK CMOs have given the advice*
- *says parents should consider not letting their children have mobile phones.*

Text B:

- *talks about radiation*
- *says what the difference is between children's and adults' vulnerability to radiation in their heads*
- *says phone companies shouldn't direct their advertising at children*
- *says there might be a minimum age introduced for mobile phone use*
- *says mobile phone masts should not be built at schools.*

12 An explanation text should be carefully structured. Look more closely at the way these texts organize their information. How do the two writers structure their texts to make their explanations clear? You might look at:

- how the information is introduced at the beginning
- the sources that are given for the information
- how ideas are linked together by connectives
- layout features that help to present information.

Text A:

Information initially introduced with general statements about usefulness of mobile phones and choice of whether to use them. Ideas linked with words like 'however' and 'because'. Bullet points in second to last paragraph help present the information; no other layout features used apart from paragraphing.

Text B:

Information initially introduced with an attention-grabbing question, followed by a statement about safety concerns. Ideas linked with words including 'but', 'until', 'so that's why'. Paragraphs are separated by spaces for clarity, important words are highlighted with bold type, and bullet points divide up important information.

Language and structure

1   Look carefully at the two texts. Try to find a sentence from each text which states the same basic message. Write down these two sentences. Is there anything you notice about differences between the two sentences, such as:

- length
- complexity
- the kind of vocabulary the writer uses?

Possible sentences:

A: *The current balance of evidence does not show health problems caused by using mobile phones.*

B: *Experts say there is no evidence to link mobiles **directly** to ill health.*

A: *The expert group has therefore recommended that in line with a precautionary approach, the widespread use of mobile phones by children (under the age of 16) should be discouraged for non-essential calls.*

B: *But now an official **government** report has found that children should definitely be careful, until more research has been carried out.*

Differences:

Text A sentences are longer than Text B ones. They are structured in a more complex way (e.g. more clauses, use of passive), and the vocabulary is more adult (e.g. longer words like 'precautionary', phrases like 'balance of evidence').

2   **a**   What clues are there in the layout and structure that Text A is aimed at an older audience?
Text in large blocks (first paragraph is very long); structured to be read as a single piece (you couldn't dip into it to find information)

   b   How can you tell from the layout *and language* that Text B is aimed at a younger audience?
Text in smaller blocks; lots of bullet points; key words in bold
Language is simpler than Text A's, and more informal:

- *shorter, simpler sentences*
- *simpler words ('be careful' as opposed to 'precautionary approach')*
- *friendly phrases like 'it's all a bit confusing'*
- *contractions like 'it's', 'can't', 'they're', 'shouldn't'.*

3   Looking more closely at Text B, can you say how you think information on websites is often presented differently?
Information is broken into short paragraphs to be easy to read on screen; bullet points divide information into small chunks; there may be pictures.

4   Explanation texts sometimes include questions. The writer of Text B does this at the beginning of paragraphs one and three. What is the purpose of these questions?
To grab the readers' attention for what they are to read next

5   Look at this statement:
Text A uses scientific language and is more formal. Text B is less scientific and more informal.
Do you agree or disagree? Write down your answer giving an example from each text to support it.
Personal opinion, but students should agree.
An acceptable answer will identify some scientific and formal language in Text A and see that Text B includes less of this. A more developed answer will also point out the use of the passive in Text A and questions and contractions in Text B.

Examples that could be used in support:

Text A scientific language: 'current balance of evidence'; 'affects brain activity'

Text A formal language: 'unrecognised health risks'; 'vulnerable'; 'should be encouraged to'; 'should be discouraged'; 'exercise their choice'

Text B less formal language: 'for a while'; 'are worried'; 'so what should you do?'; 'cut down'; 'don't'; 'shouldn't'; 'the problem is, it's all a bit confusing'

Unit 4 Instruction texts
Giving informal instructions: Telepathic Powers

Understanding the text

Before reading

1   Think about your own ability to give instructions. How clear and precise are you? If you were teaching someone to do a card trick, or to tie a school tie, how would you organize the instructions?
Put them in the order they should be followed.

2   How would you change your instructions if the audience were older or younger?
For an older audience, you could use longer, more complex sentences, and more complex language.
For a younger audience, use simpler language, shorter sentences.

3   If the audience already knew quite a bit about the topic, would that change the way you gave instructions?
Probably – especially if the instructions depended on detailed knowledge of a subject or a process. If the audience already had detailed knowledge, less explanation would be necessary.

4   Make some predictions about the text from the magic book. It is aimed at a young audience, probably aged between 9 and 14. How do you predict it will address the audience? Will it be chatty, friendly, formal, impersonal? Will it address the reader as 'you'? Will it refer to the writer as 'I' and 'me'?
Personal opinion. Probable expectations:
- *chatty, informal*
- *address reader as 'you'*
- *might not refer to writer at all.*

5   Look at the image used with the text. What does it suggest about when the book was written and who it is aimed at? Look at the way the children are sitting and how they are dressed. How would a modern image be different?
The text was written a little while ago. It is aimed at middle-class children.
The children are dressed in 1970s clothes: girls mostly in skirts, boys in shirts or T-shirts; they are sitting on the floor in a plain room. All the children are white.
A modern image might well be a photograph, not a sketch; girls would be more likely to be wearing trousers; there might be a mix of races; there would probably be a television or computer in the background.

After reading

6   In a sentence, how does the trick work?
The friend who goes out of the room knows in advance that the person doing the trick will point to a picture card just before pointing to the card that has been chosen.

7   How does the 'variation' work?
The signal is different so the cards can be placed face down: a black-backed card is used instead of a picture card, or the top right-hand corner of the card is pointed at.

8 In the picture, how can you tell who is doing the trick?

The boy has his finger on a card.

Interpreting the text

9 The writer has divided the text into short paragraphs, using some subheadings. How could the writer have organized the information to make the instructions even clearer?

By using numbers or bullet points

10 Look back at the predictions you made when you answered question 4. Write a brief review (2–3 sentences) saying whether the writer's style is similar to what you predicted. For example, is the tone more or less chatty than you expected? What other differences or similarities were there?

Personal opinion, depending on answers given to question 4. Students will probably find the style more formal and less chatty than they expected.

Language and structure

1 Instruction texts tend to use command sentences which begin with a verb, such as 'Ask one of your friends . . .'.

  a Find another command sentence in this text.

  Possible answers from the first section (there are others in the text):

  - *While he or she is out spread . . .*
  - *Now ask . . .*
  - *Explain that . . .*
  - *Emphasise that you will not . . .*

  b Find a sentence which is a statement rather than a command.

  Possible answers (there are others in the text):

  - *This is an ideal trick to perform . . .*
  - *When you point to the card chosen . . .*
  - *You do in fact have a secret signal.*
  - *But try as they might . . .*
  - *This trick can also be performed . . .*

2 The writer's style is sometimes formal. Look more closely at this paragraph:

If a picture card has been chosen as the selected card you simply point to one of the other picture cards first. Your friend will then know that the next card will be the selected one.

The first sentence starts by using the passive voice: 'If a picture card has been chosen . . .'.

  a How could this sentence be written in the active voice?

  Possible rewrite:

  If your friend has chosen a picture card, you simply point to one of the other picture cards first.

  b The final phrase 'the selected one' also sounds quite formal. Look at all of the second sentence and write it in a style which is more informal and friendly.

  Possible rewrite:

  Then your friend will know that the next card will be the one that was chosen.

3 How would the instructions for this trick be different if you were *telling* a friend about the trick, rather than giving written instructions? How would you change:

  - the overall structure
  - the sentences

- the vocabulary
- the tone?

Would you address the audience differently?

Imagine you are speaking to a friend and telling her or him about the trick. Write down what you would say. Then write a brief paragraph describing the differences between your spoken version of the trick and the written version.

The new version should be:

- *more simply structured, possibly with the instructions in the order they should be followed*
- *made up of shorter sentences, which may be less complex*
- *expressed in simpler, more informal vocabulary*
- *expressed in a friendlier, less formal tone.*

Unit 5 Descriptive texts
Describing a place: Memories of Leeds

Understanding the text

1 What does Keith Waterhouse mean when he says that 'The Horse Meat Shop . . . was always a draw'?
That he always felt drawn to it and wanted to look in its windows

2 What does he find particularly fascinating about that shop?
The fact that it was very easy to imagine the meat in the window as parts of horses

3 What was the Murder Shop? Why does he call it this?
It was a shop which sold kitchen knives and scissors. He calls it this because he thought the knives must be murder weapons.

4 How does his description of the herbalist's shop show that he is a child?
He wondered whether the 'dragon's blood' was real blood from a real dragon.

5 Why do you think Keith Waterhouse is anxious about the Board Man?
A range of answers is possible here. Some students may focus on Waterhouse's concern that his interests are unusual for a child of his age and that he might be reported for this. Others may conclude that he should be in school but is not, so is mostly concerned about being caught playing truant.

Interpreting the text

6 Which of these words best describes the way Keith Waterhouse presents himself in this extract?
curious   fascinated   childish   nervous   optimistic   young
Write a sentence explaining your choice.
Most choices could be justified:
Curious: he is fascinated by the contents of the shop windows and drawn to unusual things rather than the familiar toy shop; he likes making up explanations for the things he sees (like the display in the Murder Shop).
Fascinated: he is drawn to certain windows and stares at the things in them for a long time: the horse meat, the knives, and even the photos in the Polyfoto studio window, which he examines in detail.
Childish: he doesn't realize what the Murder Shop really is or that the 'dragon's blood' might not be the real thing.
Nervous: he thinks he has spotted the Board Man watching him, when it is really just a random passer-by.
Optimistic: no evidence for this.

Young: same evidence as for 'childish', and his mention of being 'eight or nine'.

7 How does the shopping area described feel different from town and city centres today? You might mention:

- the way the shops are organized
- what they sell
- their names
- what they look like.

Leeds then:

- *some of the shops are in tumbledown buildings*
- *different sorts of shop e.g. separate shops for horse meat and pork products*
- *the bookshop has a tray of cheap books outside*
- *some shops have old-fashioned names, e.g. Montague Burton the Tailor of Taste*
- *shops have distinctive windows, e.g. the tailor's has a row of church-style windows*
- *the Horse Meat Shop is painted red.*

Town centres now:

- *the shops are generally in well-kept buildings*
- *more shops are combined into supermarkets, general butchers, etc.*
- *more shops are chain stores, rather than independent and unique*
- *bookshops and second-hand shops usually have all their goods inside now*
- *shop names are shorter, e.g. Burton's, Debenhams, etc.*
- *shop windows look fairly uniform, with large panes of clear glass*
- *butchers' shops are usually white, with no suggestion of blood.*

Language and structure

1 One way writers can create vivid description is by using lists of details within sentences, for example:
little saucers containing powdered ginger, bee salve, prune and senna mixture, licorice root . . .

   a Write down another example of this 'list' technique in the text.
   Marble slabs of pies and pasties and polonies

   b What is the effect of this way of describing things?
   It suggests how much there was to look at and how fascinating it was.

2 Descriptive texts may also use words describing colour and texture. Write down some examples of Keith Waterhouse's words or phrases which use the senses of sight and touch.

Sight:

- *unappetising purplish joints*
- *lumps of yellow fat*
- *painted in a vivid red, like blood*
- *good for a stare*
- *I would feast my eyes*
- *these gastronomic displays were visually pleasing.*

Touch:

- *I could finger the old books*
- *scoop out an egg-shaped quantity of meat*
- *wedge the egg into the aperture.*

3   The text uses mostly long, complex sentences, with many subordinate clauses. Why do you think Keith Waterhouse uses these rather than short, simple sentences?

Short sentences would chop up the text and make it feel more abrupt. The long sentences help to build up lots of detail, and give a slow rhythm which reflects the mood of the writer looking back on his childhood obsessions.

4   This is a personal piece of writing. In what ways does the writer use language which is personal – showing us the thoughts and feelings of a young child?

Personal language:

- *I liked to hear my mother tell me . . .*
- *I imagined in my confused way . . .*
- *. . . before I would dare venture inside*
- *which always left me puzzling . . .*
- *I thought I spotted . . .*
- *it did set me wondering . . .*
- *I was beginning to hanker after . . .*
- *. . . as I could readily acknowledge in moments of insight.*

5   Writers can use imagery to bring their descriptions alive. Using your own words, write down the picture the following phrases create in your mind. The key words of each are highlighted. Does the image recall something you have seen or experienced yourself?

Possible answers:

Image	The picture it creates
a Painted in a vivid red, **like blood**	*A dark red, sinister and possibly even wet, emphasizing the gory nature of the butcher's shop*
b The **stew** of tumbledown premises	*It's as if the buildings are made of bits jumbled together like food in a stew; messy and slightly off-putting*
c The **bisected** veal, ham and egg pies	*Sounds scientific and clinical, as if the pie is laid on a slab in a laboratory and cut precisely in half*

6   How would Keith Waterhouse's writing seem without all the description? Write a one-paragraph factual version which focuses on what he does and where he goes, rather than on describing what he sees. Make it as bald and non-descriptive as you can.

Then write a sentence describing how you approached the task and what the final text is like.

Possible rewrite:

I always went to look at the Horse Meat Shop, at the side of the Market, because it was so easy to believe that the meat in the window was horse. My mother said it had to look different from the other butchers' shops, by law. I liked to look at the herbalist's shop too. There was also the Murder Shop, with knives and scissors that I thought must be for killing people. I used to finger the books in the box outside the second-hand bookshop, but I didn't dare go in for years. There was a photo shop which used the latest technology and I liked looking to see which pictures in the window showed people blinking. I loved looking at the products in the pork shops' windows and always wondered how they had been made – and while I was musing on this one day, I thought I saw the Board Man watching me. I soon realized that it wasn't him, but I did wonder how I would explain what I had been looking at if it was the Board Man – I had ignored the toy shops and gazed at all these other places, including a tailor's shop because I fancied a suit. It was a strange way for a child to behave, but I must have been a funny child.

Most students will approach the task as a sort of summary: the original is so full of description that it needs to be completely rewritten to leave it out. The final texts will be much shorter, less detailed, and less evocative than the original.

Year 8 units

Unit 6 Recounts to entertain
Newspaper recount: Flying Solo

Understanding the text

1 Where did the incident take place?
Canterbury Airfield, Kent

2 Why had the pilot left the plane?
To get the cover for the battery which he had been recharging

3 What were his first thoughts when he noticed the plane had disappeared?
He thought someone had stolen the plane.

4 How were the whereabouts of the plane discovered?
Another aircraft spotted it.

5 What is the pilot's:
- name
  Glyn Hughes
- age
  48
- family
  married, with one child
- job?
  runs an electronics business

6 Now look at the way the writer organizes the story. Which of the following questions does the article answer first: Who? When? What (happened)? Why? Where? Which of these questions gets answered last? Put the five 'W' questions in the order in which they are answered in the article. Number them 1 to 5.
Possible answer:
1 – what happened (plane took off without pilot)
2 – when (after the pilot hopped out)
3 – who (Glyn Hughes)
4 – where (Canterbury Airfield, Kent)
5 – why (not revealed by Civil Aviation Authority report)

Interpreting the text

7 Look at the diagram that accompanies the news story. Working in pairs, one person should use the diagram to explain to his or her partner exactly what happened with the aircraft. Make the explanation as clear as possible. The other person should listen and then say how clear the recount was. How could the speaker have structured the story more clearly?
Personal opinion. Students may feel that the story should be told once only, rather than once in outline and then again in greater detail, as in the article.

8 Look at how much detail the picture adds to the story.
   a Does the diagram contain all the essential pieces of information? Are there any other details you might

have included?

Personal opinion. The diagram seems to contain all the essentials, but some students might feel that names and so on should be added.

b Do you think the diagram is important for fully understanding what happened? Explain why.

Personal opinion. The diagram helps to clarify what route the plane took and the sequence of events.

9 Throughout the story the writer refers to 'Glyn' (using his first name). Is this more or less formal than you might expect? What effect would it have had if the writer had referred to him as 'Hughes' or 'Mr Hughes'?

It seems informal, as if the writer knows the pilot personally. 'Mr Hughes' would sound more formal. 'Hughes' would sound like a police report.

10 Towards the end of the article a pilot is quoted, talking about Glyn. Read what he says. What does he imply about Glyn and why the plane might have taken off without him?

He implies that Glyn is a rather careless pilot. He suggests that Glyn's report of events is wrong and that he actually caused the accident, for example, by leaving the brake off.

Language and structure

1 Look more closely at the headline. Even if this wasn't printed in large lettering, you would probably know that it is a newspaper headline. What features does it have which are typical of news headlines?

You might comment on:

- punctuation

   None, just a capital at the beginning

- choice of vocabulary

   Simple; uses the present tense

- words that are left out.

   The word 'a' is left out twice where it would be used in a normal sentence.

2 News stories usually start with a topic sentence, which sets the tone of the story. Why do you think the writer uses the verb 'hurtled' in this topic sentence? Think of another verb he might have used.

'Hurtled' is used as a dramatic word, to make the plane's movement sound dangerous.

Other possible words: dashed, rushed, tore, whizzed, zoomed

3 Look at the fifth paragraph. Why do you think the writer says 'cops' rather than 'police'?

It fits with the article's informal style.

4 **a** What other examples are there of informal and vivid language?

  Possible examples:

- *hopped out*
- *dashed*
- *wrecked*
- *fearing a roasting*
- *a married dad.*

 b What do these examples of informal and vivid vocabulary tell you about the writer's view of his audience? What does he think they want from the newspaper?

  The writer expects his audience to be reading for light entertainment – the informal language helps to give the article a jokey tone.

5 Look more closely at the way the writer uses punctuation to help the reader understand his story. Use the questions below to comment on some punctuation used in this text.

a In the first paragraph, why does the writer place a hyphen between 'last' and 'minute'? Would it make any difference if the hyphen were left out?

It makes it clear that the phrase 'last-minute' is intended (meaning 'done at the last minute'). Without the hyphen, the words could be read separately, giving the meaning 'a last, minute (i.e. final, detailed) check'.

b Look at the start of this sentence:

Glyn, a pilot of eight years' experience, was about to make his return flight . . .

Explain why the writer uses two commas around the phrase 'a pilot of eight years' experience'. Can you think of a different way he might have written the same ideas, using full stops rather than commas?

The writer uses commas to make it clear that this is not the main sentence but extra information about Glyn.

Possible rewrite:

Glyn was a pilot of eight years' experience. He was about to make his return flight . . .

c Look at this sentence:

One pilot said: 'Glyn's a colourful character who's had his share of incidents – I wouldn't lend him my plane.'

Why do you think the writer has chosen to separate the ideas with a dash rather than a full stop? What effect does it have?

It makes it clearer that the two ideas are connected, and makes it sound like speech.

6 This activity helps you with note-making skills. Use a form like the one below to build up a picture of what happened to the mysterious aircraft. Fill it in using details from the *Sun* article.

Self-Flying Aircraft Factsheet

What do we know about what happened, where and when?

What *The plane turned, took off without a pilot and crashed a mile away from the airfield.*

Where *Canterbury Airfield, Kent*

When *After the pilot hopped out to make a last-minute check*

What do we know about the person in control of the plane?

He is a 48 year-old London businessman; he had been flying for eight years; he hired the plane for an afternoon; he is married; he has a child; he runs his own electronics business.

What questions are left unanswered?

How it happened that the plane turned and took off

Where the missing battery cover was and whether it was found

Personal recount: Going Surfing

Understanding the text

1 How can you tell that Bill Bryson is nervous about boogie boarding?

He asks a lot of questions about what it is and the dangers involved.

2 What happens to him when he first tries to surf?

He sinks.

3 How can you tell from Glenn's reaction that 'bluebottles' are dangerous?

He looks alarmed at once.

4 Why do you think Deirdre does not tell him the full truth about the 'bluebottle'?

Personal opinion. It is probably because she does not want to alarm him and make him panic.

Interpreting the text

5 As you read the text, you probably didn't expect that Bill Bryson would be able to surf successfully. How does his ironic tone help us guess in advance that his attempts will be unsuccessful?

His repeated questions show that he knows nothing about boogie boarding, and that he is nervous; he mentions his lack of experience of the sea and plays up the stories of dangerous incidents from the past; his tone implies that it won't be as simple as Deirdre makes it look.

6 Which parts of the text did you find funniest, and why?

Personal opinion. All answers should be backed up with reasons.

Language and structure

1 **a** Look at the first section of the text. This sets the situation up for what happens later. Look at the range of sentence functions the writer uses. Try to find an example of:

- a statement

'Oh, it's fun.'

- a question

'What is boogie boarding exactly?'

- an imperative (or command)

'But don't worry.'

- a minor sentence (a sentence without a verb).

'Couple of months at least.'

(There are other examples in the text.)

b In this early section, how does the use of questions make us want to read on?

We want to read on to find out the answers.

2 The later sections use some complex sentences to explain the action. Find an example of a complex sentence that packs in a lot of detail.

Possible answer (there are others in the text):

There followed a half hour in which the two of them watched first with guarded amusement, then a kind of astonishment, and finally something not unlike pity, as I repeatedly vanished beneath the waves and was scraped over an area of ocean floor roughly the size of Polk County, Iowa.

3 Although recounts are often written in chronological order, Bill Bryson covers a number of time sequences in this extract. The first section describes him first hearing about boogie boarding. The next section moves forward in time three hours. Then he goes back in time for accounts of events in 1935 and 1938, before continuing with the description of his time at the beach.

a Find the connecting words which he uses to show the shifts to different times.

Three hours later

In 1935

Three years later

b How might he have introduced the flashback to 1935 in a different way?

Over sixty years ago . . .

c How does this use of different time sequences help to create humour?

Talking about dangerous things that happened so long ago shows how scared Bill Bryson is.

4   Like many humorous writers, Bill Bryson uses similes and exaggeration, like this:

Simile

It looked unprepossessing, like a blue condom with strings attached

Exaggeration

I was scraped over an area of ocean floor roughly the size of Polk County, Iowa

He also uses some memorable phrasing, with metaphors like this:

. . . wading into a rollercoaster of water.

Each of these techniques adds to the comic effect. Find a sentence or phrase using one of these techniques, which you think is particularly effective. Write it down, and comment on why you think it adds humour to the text.

Similes:

* *. . . jumped aboard and sank like an anvil*

Exaggeration:

* *. . . at a point anywhere from four feet to a mile and a quarter distant*
* *. . . nearly naked and half drowned*

Memorable phrasing / metaphors:

* *the briny drink*
* *a big, languorous wave*
* *vulnerable and abraded*

Students will probably think that these expressions add humour to the text because of the vivid, comical images they conjure up.

5   Look at the newspaper account Deirdre Macken writes. Her style is quite different from Bill Bryson's and also comic. How does she write differently from him? You might mention:

* the length of her sentences
* whether she uses the same range of sentences as Bill Bryson
* the way she describes Bryson's character
* the way she describes things he has *not* done
* whether her account is more formal or informal.

The sentences are all short apart from the last one.

She writes mostly in the present tense while he writes in the past.

She uses statements, but not questions, imperatives or minor sentences.

She suggests that Bryson has taken no trouble to inform himself about possible dangers.

She builds up the mention of the things he has not done in a series of three sentences, each one longer than the last.

Her account seems more formal than Bryson's.

Unit 7 Autobiographical recounts
Healing the Horses

Understanding the text

1   How can you tell that the journey to reach the horses has been hard work for the narrator?
He says he is glad when they reach 'the flat land at the bottom', which implies they have been walking on a long slope. His arms feel stretched: he has been carrying something heavy for a long time. He is sweating.

2   What signs are there that the horses are old?

Their coats have a lot of grey in them, their eyes are very sunken, and the marks on their teeth (which are supposed to show their age) have worn away.

3 How do the horses show that they like Mr Skipton?

They prance around him and try to knock his cap over his eyes.

4 What is the problem with the first horse's mouth?

The outside edges of the back teeth are overgrown. They are irritating the insides of the mouth and the tongue.

5 What is the problem with the second horse's mouth?

An upper back tooth is overlapping a lower one, and has overgrown into a long sharp spike that stabs into the gums below.

Interpreting the text

6 Look at the men's conversation about how long it is since the horses last did any work. What is implied about Mr Skipton's past experiences, and his feelings for the horses?

Mr Skipton says they were slaves together, suggesting that he worked with them when he was younger, in a tough situation about which they had no choice. He clearly has a strong relationship with the horses and feels that he owes them a quiet retirement now they are no longer in that situation.

7 What impression do you get of James Herriott from the extract? Think about:
- how he gets on with Mr Skipton
- how he deals with the horses' problems
- how he speaks.

He seems a very professional vet, asking questions to find out as much as possible about the animals. He doesn't make much conversation with Mr Skipton about anything else, perhaps respecting his privacy.
He deals with the horses' problems on the spot.
He speaks in a fairly professional way, but is friendly. He doesn't have a Yorkshire accent like Mr Skipton.

8 The text is based on real-life people and events. But would it be possible to see it purely as a made-up story? What features do you notice in this autobiographical writing which you might also expect in fiction (for example, a novel set in the countryside)? Aim to find two features.

Possible features:
- *dialogue*
- *description of the countryside*
- *description of the horses.*

Language and structure

1 While James Herriott speaks in standard English, Mr Skipton uses a number of Yorkshire dialect words and structures.
- **a** Find a word he uses which we would not expect to find in standard English.
- **b** Write down what you think the word means.

Possible answers:
- *aye – yes*
- *daft – silly*
- *awd – old*
- *lakin' – leaping, playing*
- *t' – the*

- *grand – great*
- *ailed – been ill*
- *owt – at all*
- *champin' – chewing*
- *summat – something.*

2   Now look again at James Herriott's own spoken words – such as: 'They're in a nice spot, Mr Skipton.' Which of the following statements do you think best explains the way the writer presents his own language?

a   The way James Herriott speaks shows that he comes from a different background from Mr Skipton.

b   It shows that James Herriott is an outsider in this area – he does not belong here.

c   James Herriott celebrates the way people speak in their own dialects.

d   James Herriott is presented as 'posh' in his language.

Write a sentence explaining your choice.

Possible answers:

a, b, d – James Herriott's speech doesn't include any Yorkshire dialect words, which suggests that he is from a different background, a different area or is 'posh'.

c – this appears to be true but is not demonstrated by Herriott's presentation of his own speech.

3   Yorkshire dialect also uses certain phrases and structures, like these:

retired like   an' all   t'other (rather than 'the other')

Take the following three examples and write them in the standard English dialect used by James Herriott:

a   'Aye, just lakin' about down here, retired like.'

   'Yes, just playing about down here, sort of retired.'

b   'They've earned it an' all.'

   'They've earned it too.'

c   'Now have a look at t'other.'

   'Now have a look at the other one.'

4   Think about the way you have rewritten the dialect expressions in standard English for question 3. Try to describe how you can tell the difference between Yorkshire dialect and standard English. Use the list below to help you – it gives some examples of the ways different dialects may vary from standard English.

- Irregular agreement between subject and verb (e.g. *we was*).
- Irregular formation of the past tense (e.g. *it **were** finished*).
- Different vocabulary from standard English (e.g. *bairn* instead of *child*).
- Phrases which we would not find in standard English.
- Different use of pronouns and prepositions (e.g. *we saw **them** horses*).
- Running two words of standard English together to make a new word (e.g. *we saw **t'old** man*).

Start your comment like this:

Example a) seems like regional dialect rather than standard English because . . .

a – different vocabulary from standard English ('aye' for 'yes', 'lakin'' for 'playing'); phrase we would not find in standard English ('retired, like' for 'sort of retired')

b – different vocabulary from standard English ('an' all' for 'too / as well')

c – running two words of standard English together to make a new word ('t'other' for 'the other')

Personal recount: Relative Values

Understanding the text

1 Write down two facts we learn from the article about her parents' background – one about Des'ree's mother and another about her father.

Possible answers (there are others in the text):

Father:

- *born in Barbados*
- *came to London in 1960s to study accountancy*
- *quiet and reserved*
- *was a talented cricketer as a child*
- *loved jazz.*

Mother:

- *came from Guyana*
- *came to London to study nursing*
- *ambitious.*

2 Why did the family move to Barbados?

The parents wanted their children to experience life in the West Indies.

3 Why did the father's family not get on with Des'ree's mother?

Des'ree says it is because of a natural tendency for people from Guyana and Barbados not to get on with each other. It might also be because Des'ree's mother didn't want to live in the family home.

4 How did Des'ree's attitude to her father change in Barbados?

She decided that he was weak.

5 When did Des'ree last see her father?

Last Christmas

Interpreting the text

6 How can you tell that Des'ree's family is important to her?

The whole article is about her relationship with them, and she never mentions friends or anyone else.

7 By the end of the article she says: 'I'm not angry any more.' How has her understanding of her father changed? Can we see this change developing as her recount goes along?

By the end she has come to understand her father, rather than just blaming him for his mistakes.

At the beginning she seems to admire him – the way he cooks, for example.

When she talks about their time in Barbados, she seems dismissive of his excuses for not wanting to move out of his parents' house. Then when her parents are splitting up, she describes her father as weak, and like a stranger to her. She expresses her anger and disappointment in him and makes it clear she only stays in touch with him because her mother wants her to.

Describing last Christmas, she says that the conversations she and her sister had with him have taught her that he was too easy-going and so didn't do the things in life he felt he should have – so he is perhaps more to be pitied than despised.

8 How would you describe the tone of the writer?

bitter   angry   disappointed   resentful   accepting

Write down the word that you think is most suitable, and then write a sentence explaining why you have chosen it.

Personal opinion. A good answer will back up the opinion with evidence from the text. The best word for the overall tone of the text would be 'disappointed' or 'accepting', although the other emotions are expressed at some points in the text.

9 Some people might say that Des'ree's recount seems biased rather than factual – that it is impossible for her to describe her life and family in an objective way. Do you agree or disagree? Say why.

Personal opinion. A good answer will back up the opinion with evidence from the text. Some students may argue that it is impossible to be objective about your own close family.

10 Personal recounts tend to contain both facts and opinions. Use a table like the one below to sort out the differences between facts and opinions in this text.

Possible answers:

Facts about her father	Opinions about her father
<ul><li>born in Barbados</li><li>came to London in 1960s to study accountancy</li><li>quiet and reserved</li><li>was a talented cricketer as a child</li><li>loved jazz</li><li>looked a lot older after ten years away</li></ul>	<ul><li>left most things up to her mother</li><li>happy and relaxed in the West Indies</li><li>made excuses not to leave his parents' house</li><li>weak</li><li>too easy-going</li></ul>
Facts about her mother	**Opinions about her mother**
<ul><li>came from Guyana</li><li>came to London to study nursing</li><li>ambitious</li></ul>	<ul><li>pushed and encouraged her husband</li><li>unhappy in Barbados</li><li>wanted to be composed for her daughters</li></ul>

Facts about Des'ree
<ul><li>grew up in southeast London</li><li>went to live in Barbados with parents for a time</li><li>noticed there that the family was not as happy as before</li><li>felt jittery at the prospect of the parents' marriage ending</li><li>stayed in touch with her father for her mother's sake</li><li>went to St Lucia to see him last Christmas</li><li>told him then how she felt</li></ul>

Why don't we gain any direct opinions of Des'ree herself?

Because she is writing the piece focusing on her feelings about her parents, rather than about herself

Language and structure

1 Some parts of Des'ree's text feel quite formal; other parts seem informal.

    a Find three examples of formal words or phrases and three of informal ones. Try to explain why you think they are formal or informal. An example is done for you.

        Formal style

        Example: *there is a natural antipathy*

        Comment: *'antipathy' is an unfamiliar, technical word.*

Informal style

Example: *so we upped sticks and moved to Barbados*

Comment: *'upped sticks' is a chatty expression which you might use in spoken English rather than a written text.*

Possible answers (there are others in the text):

Formal phrases:

- *'he had very domineering parents' – 'domineering' is quite a technical word*
- *'my mum was a little more apprehensive' – 'apprehensive' is a formal, controlled word*
- *'about to be severed' – 'severed' is a technical, formal word*
- *'stopped communicating with him' – 'communicating' is a formal word.*

Informal phrases:

- *'kept up his links with his homeland' – 'kept up' is informal, chatty*
- *'meeting his old buddies' – 'buddies' is informal*
- *'didn't pretend everything was okay' – 'okay' is informal*
- *'started to feel jittery' – 'jittery' is informal.*

b The writer refers to her parents as 'Mum' and 'Dad'. What effect would it have if she used the phrases 'my mother' and 'my father' instead?

It would make the whole text sound more formal. It might make her sound more detached from the situations she is describing and in her feelings for her parents.

2 Des'ree uses a variety of sentences and joins them together with connectives. Her recount moves backwards and forwards in time. At the start of some paragraphs she uses connectives to help the reader follow the sequence of her writing.

Look at these three examples of connectives used at the beginning of paragraphs, and describe the purpose of each one. Use the prompt list on the next page to help you.

Various answers are possible, but these are the 'best fits':

Example of connective	Purpose of the connective
After (paragraph 4)	To move us forward in time
So (paragraph 5)	To show the effect of something that has happened
One day (paragraph 8)	To move us forward in time

Possible purposes of connectives

- to move us back in time
- to give an illustration or example
- to show the effect of something that has happened
- to move us forward in time
- to summarize or generalize
- to move to a different setting.

3 Look at the two examples below, where Des'ree uses semi-colons within her sentences:

Dad was born in Barbados and came over here in the 1960s to study accountancy; my mother came over from Guyana at the same time to study nursing.

He took it quietly; maybe he hadn't anticipated that I would tell him that.

a How would the effect have been different if Des'ree had used a full stop instead of the semi-colon?

It would have made the two ideas more separate, reducing the connection between them.

b How does the semi-colon help Des'ree to express her meaning more precisely?

It helps her to connect the ideas and show that they are strongly related. In the first sentence, she is relating her parents' backgrounds to show their similarity; in the second, she is commenting on his reaction (or lack of it) and trying to see why it was so.

Unit 8 Information texts
Technical information: Exploded Drawings

Understanding the text

1 What is an exploded drawing for?

To show how the separate parts of something fit together

2 How does the writer help readers to know what they should have learned by the end of the unit?

There is a heading at the top of the page: 'By the end of this spread, you should be able to', with a bullet point underneath.

3 Why do the drawings need to show the separate parts of objects?

To make it clear how they fit together

4 Look at the formal words below. Think of a different word or phrase that the writer might have used:

a how a product is **assembled**

put together, fitted together, made up

b views of the same **components**.

parts, bits

Interpreting the text

5 In information texts, paragraphs are often organized so that each contains one piece of information. Look at the structure of this text. It is written in short paragraphs. Use a grid like the one below to say what each of these paragraphs is about.

Paragraph	Topic
1	*What an exploded drawing is for*
2	*More about what an exploded drawing is*
3	*How an exploded drawing should be drawn to be useful*
4	*Asking the reader to look at the examples*
5	*Another example*

6 Using your completed grid to help you, decide which of these statements (a–d) you most agree with.

a The text gives a lot of examples of exploded drawings.

b The text starts with an example of an exploded drawing, and then shows how these can work in other subject areas.

c The first paragraph introduces the topic. The second gives more detail. The rest of the paragraphs provide examples.

d The first paragraph introduces the topic. Paragraphs 2 and 3 give more information. Paragraph 4 gets the reader thinking about examples. Paragraph 5 gives a further example.

Write a sentence explaining your choice.

Most students should choose d.

7 On a scale of 1 (low) to 5 (high), how helpful do you find the layout of the page in making the information clear? Write a sentence saying how you think the layout could be improved.

Personal opinion. The diagrams could be more integrated with the text to make the information clearer.

8 Think about the audience for this text. Is it aimed at people who know very little about the subject, people who have a background understanding, or experts? Write a sentence explaining how you can tell.

It is aimed at people who know something about the subject; it doesn't explain any of the technical terms.

Language and structure

1 Working with a partner, tell her or him about the information you have read in this text. Your partner should make notes about the way you describe the information.

In particular, listen out for:

● informal words

● longer sentences than are used in the book

● fillers (*er, erm*) and repetition – these are known as **non-fluency features**.

All of these features should be found as they are typical of normal speech.

2 Like many information texts, this textbook uses quite formal language. It includes some technical words: *perspective, three-dimensional, exploded, interior.*

a Choose one of these technical terms and – using your own words – write down what you think it means.

Possible answers:

Perspective: showing something in a picture so that the parts that are further away from you look smaller

Three-dimensional: looking as if it stands out from the page, rather than being completely flat

Exploded: taken apart to show how it fits together

Interior: inside

b Describe something the writer might have done to help a reader who does *not* know that word.

Personal opinion. Students may suggest:

● *adding an explanation in brackets after the word*

● *including a glossary*

● *including diagrams to show what is meant by the terms.*

3 Information texts tend to be written mostly in statements. This text includes a question:

Which illustration do you think would be . . .?

Why do you think the writer includes a question at this point?

To make the readers think about what they are looking at and to make sure they are trying to understand the explanation.

4 Look at this sentence:

The following illustration has been drawn using a different exploded drawing method.

a The writer has written this in the passive voice. He or she could have written it in the active voice using the pronoun 'we'. Write an active version of the sentence, starting with 'We'.

We have drawn the following illustration using a different exploded drawing method.

b Why do you think the writer chose the passive form?

Because it is not important to say who did the drawing

Unit 9 Explanation texts
Explaining a process: Why is the Sky Blue . . . ?

Understanding the text

1 Pick out two sentences from the text which you think best answer the reader's question.

So the sky is blue because it is full of tiny floating particles of dust that scatter the blue parts of sunlight. In turn the sun gets redder at sunset as the light travels through more atmosphere, so more light is scattered and only red gets through.

2 What was the relationship of John Tyndall to Michael Faraday?

He was director of the Royal Institution after Faraday.

3 What was Tyndall particularly good at?

Thinking up demonstrations

Interpreting the text

4 How does Adam Hart-Davis use layout to make his explanation easy to follow?

He divides the explanation into four sections: general information about Tyndall; a list of what is needed; how to do the activity; and the explanation of how it works.

5 How might the writing itself have been made easier to follow? If you had been the editor of the page, would you have added bullet points, shorter paragraphs, more subheadings, words in bold or italics? Write a brief paragraph about how you might make the explanation even clearer.

Personal opinion. Students might suggest that dividing the 'What to do' and 'How it works' sections into shorter paragraphs or bullet points would make them easier to follow.

6 Why do you think Adam Hart-Davis includes historical information about John Tyndall?

Possible answers:
- *because Tyndall thought up the demonstration*
- *because Adam Hart-Davis is as interested in scientists as in explaining science.*

7 By the end of the text, do you feel that the original question has been fully answered? Are there any further questions it makes you want to ask?

Personal opinion. Students may want explanation of the last statement: that if there were no dust or water in the air, the sky would be black.

Language and structure

1 Adam Hart-Davis uses a number of sentence functions in his text. Find an example of:
- a command
  Possible answers:
  have a go . . .
  see how it works
  start by filling . . .
  balance the torch . . .
  add about a quarter teaspoon . . .

give it a good stir

look at the side . . .

look at the end . . .

keep adding milk

watch your sky . . .

- a statement.

  Possible answers:

  why the sky is blue was first discovered by . . .

  Tyndall was very good at . . .

  the water should look slightly blue

  this is your sky . . .

  you should see a yellow sun

  Any of the sentences in the last paragraph

2 a Write down a phrase or sentence in which Adam Hart-Davis uses the past tense.

Possible answers:

- *why the sky is blue was first discovered . . .*
- *Tyndall was very good at thinking up demonstrations*
- *Tyndall noticed that when . . .*
- *but when he tried to do this . . .*
- *he realised that the only reason why . . .*

b Write down a phrase or sentence in which Adam Hart-Davis uses the present tense.

Possible answers (there are others in the text):

- *this is your sky; it is not very blue . . .*
- *he realised that the only reason that you can 'see' beams of light is . . .*
- *and this is exactly what is happening . . .*
- *when a ray of light hits a milk particle . . .*
- *small particles scatter blue light . . .*

3 The text is structured like this:

1 introduction

2 ingredients

3 instruction

4 explanation

a Why is section 1 written mostly in the past tense?

Because it is mostly about Tyndall, who is a historical figure

b Why is the last sentence of this section in the present tense?

Because it is about an activity the reader can do now

c Why is section 3 in the present tense?

Because it is describing what should happen as the reader does the activity

d Why does section 4 start in the past and then change to the present tense?

Because it starts off talking about what Tyndall discovered in the past, and then goes on to explain the general reasons why this is so, describing a situation that is still true and happening now

4 Look at the instructions in section 3. Write down two connectives the writer uses to show that one instruction follows another.

Next; now

5 Explanation texts can be written in quite an informal tone. Adam Hart-Davis does this in two main ways.

   a He addresses the reader directly, like this:

     *This means that when **you** look at the scattered light from the side of the tank, it is slightly blue . . .*

     Write this sentence so that it is more formal and does not refer directly to the reader.

     Possible rewrite:

     This means that when scattered light is seen from the end of the tank, it is slightly blue . . .

   b He also uses some informal vocabulary, like this:

     *When a ray of light **hits** a milk particle it **bounces off in all directions . . .***

     Try to write this in a more formal, technical style, by paying particular attention to the highlighted words.

     Possible rewrite:

     When a ray of light strikes a milk particle, it is reflected at many angles . . .

   c Why do you think Adam Hart-Davis chooses this informal tone?

     To make his explanation friendly-sounding and easy to understand

6 The last section of the text explains how something works. It uses a number of connectives to show how one idea relates to another. Look at the list of connectives below and describe what part each one plays in the text. The first example is done for you.

Connective	Function
And	*Shows how this idea continues from the last one*
This means	*Shows how this idea comes out of the last one*
So	*Shows how this idea comes out of the last one*
In turn	*Shows that this idea is a further consequence of an earlier one*
If	*Shows that what is said next is a supposition*

7 Look at the way the writer uses verbs:

*Look at the end of the fish tank and you **should** see a yellow sun . . .*

How would the effect be different if he had said you *will*, *might*, or *could* see?

   a Which of these modal verbs feels *most* definite?

     Will

   b Which feels *least* definite?

     Might

8 How would you redesign the page to make the process clearer for a younger audience? How would you use images differently? Would you organize the text in a different way?

Map out a new page design for the website. Then write a brief paragraph explaining why your changes would make the information easier for a young reader to understand.

Personal opinion. Students may suggest combining the text with the images so that numbered pictures are integrated with the instructions for the activity, and with the explanation.

Year 9 units

Unit 10 Media recounts
News article: An Ealing Comedy of Errors

Understanding the text

1 For how long had police known about the plot?

Two months

2 How many people were arrested?

12

3 How many members of the public were in the Dome when the raid began?

More than 60

4 Using the whole article, write a topic sentence which explains to a new reader what happened at the Dome on 7 November 2000.

Possible answer:

On 7 November 2000, police prevented a gang of criminals from stealing some rare diamonds from an exhibition in the Millennium Dome.

Interpreting the text

5 Quite a lot of readers may not understand the headline if they do not know about Ealing comedies.

   a Why do you think the editor of this page wants to compare the robbery to comedy films?

      To make the failed robbery attempt sound funny and ham-fisted, like something in a comedy film

   b What does this tell you about the audience the newspaper is aimed at?

      It is probably aimed more at middle-aged people than young ones, as middle-aged people will be more familiar with the films.

6 Look at the way the robbers are presented in the article. Are they shown as:

   daring   foolish   dangerous   unlucky?

   Choose one or two words that best sum up the way the article presents them. Find some examples from the article to support your choices.

   All answers are possible; good answers will be backed up with evidence from the text.

7 Newspaper reports often blend fact with opinion. Look at this sentence from the article:

   But a gritty drama of criminal daring swiftly turned into something more akin to an Ealing comedy.

   How far is this sentence fact and how far is it opinion? Can you tell the writer's attitude from it? If you were to write the information in a purely factual sentence, how would you express it?

   Fact: a criminal act swiftly turned into something more comical

   Opinion: gritty drama; daring; more akin to an Ealing comedy

   Possible rewrite: But the criminals' plans were swiftly turned into a funny scene.

8 The writers describe it as 'the astonishing raid attempt'. Why do you think they include the word 'astonishing'?

   To emphasize the daring of the plan and to grab the reader's attention

9 Some readers may feel that the article contains quite a lot of the authors' own opinions, and also that it makes the raid seem glamorous. Do you agree?

Possible example words / phrases:

- *like a scene from The Sweeney*
- *powerful engines*
- *gritty*
- *daring*
- *astonishing*
- *could easily have been inspired by the latest James Bond blockbuster.*

Most students will think these words make the raid sound glamorous: they relate it to television and film, and words like 'daring' and 'astonishing' sound admiring.

Language and structure

1 We normally expect the first paragraph of a newspaper article to use a topic sentence – a sentence that tells us the whole story (answering the questions *who, what, where, when?*).

    a How is this paragraph different from what we might expect?

       It does not sum up the story, but gives an impression of the drama of the event.

    b How does the writer try to grab our attention with this opening? Do you think it works?

       The writer grabs our attention by making the events sound dramatic. It does work – mainly because it uses dramatic language and the powerful image of the JCB smashing into the Dome.

2 The structure of the article is:

- first describe the raid
- then give quotations from eyewitnesses.

    a Why does the writer include quotations from eyewitnesses? How would the story be different without them?

       The quotations make the story seem real, and show how many people were around when it happened. Without them, there would be less reaction to the events in the story and it might not be as dramatic.

    b Look at these statements by witnesses:

       i *I heard this enormous crashing noise* (eyewitness)

       ii *It was very scary* (Mandy Sylvester)

       iii *Our concern was the safety of our visitors and the people who work at The Dome* (David James)

       Which of these statements:

- feels most informal? How can you tell?

       i and ii are the most informal: i uses 'this' where formal English would use 'an'; ii uses 'scary' where formal English would use 'frightening'.

- feels most formal? How can you tell?

       iii is the most formal: it is a much longer, more controlled sentence. 'Our concern was' is a very formal phrase.

3 David James says:

Steps were taken throughout to ensure that our visitors were not put at risk.

This uses the passive voice ('Steps were taken').

    a How could the same idea have been expressed using the active voice, starting like this: 'We . . .'

       We took steps throughout to ensure that our visitors were not put at risk.

    b What difference does using the passive voice make?

       It makes it sound more formal; it does not say who took the steps.

Newsaper investigation: The Lancashire Cat Mystery

Understanding the text

1 What is the name of the village where the incidents are taking place?

Lumb

2 How many cats have disappeared so far?

15

3 What three different theories are there about where the cats are disappearing to?

The theories are that the cats might have been:

- *taken for the fur trade*
- *killed by a cat killer*
- *sold to research laboratories.*

4 What was the first case of cats disappearing?

Three rare pedigree Bengal cats vanished on 2 November.

5 How many cats disappeared on the worst night?

Three

Interpreting the text

6 Not all newspaper articles are meant to be taken entirely seriously. As you read this article, did you feel that it was a serious news story? Explain your answer.

Students may think the structure and vocabulary ('baffling riddle', 'rumour and counter-rumour') seem too serious for the subject matter, and the writer is trying to make the story sound mysterious.

7 We expect newspaper headings to be short and punchy. This one is not. Unusually, it uses two sentences.

   a What is the headline writer aiming to achieve?

   Personal opinion. Students may feel that the headline emphasizes what a small story it is, and suggests it is unimportant and slightly amusing.

   b How well do you think it works?

   Personal opinion. Good answers will give a reason.

   c Think of a headline in a more conventional style.

   Alternative headlines should be written mostly in nouns, and include 'Lancashire', 'vanishing' or 'vanish' and 'cats', e.g.

   Lancashire village's vanishing cats mystery

   Cats vanish from Lancs. village

8 If this were a front page news article, we would expect it to begin with a topic sentence summarizing the whole story.

   a Why do you think it does not do that?

   To give atmosphere – it focuses on atmosphere instead of information.

   b Write a topic sentence which would work as a summary.

   Possible answer:

   In the past two weeks, 15 cats have vanished from the village of Lumb in Lancashire.

9 What can you tell about the writer's attitude to the events? Can you tell anything also about his attitude to his readers (e.g. does he know the kind of story they like, does he aim chiefly to entertain rather than inform them)?

Choose a statement from those below which best sums up what we can say about the writer's attitude.

Then write a sentence explaining your choice.

a   It is impossible to tell what the writer's attitude is.

b   The writer is genuinely concerned.

c   The writer treats it as something of a joke.

Personal opinion. Students may feel that c is the most appropriate answer and the writer is aiming to entertain rather than inform readers. Good answers will back up opinion with evidence from the text.

10   How does the writer make readers want to keep reading on? You might mention:

- the headline
- the opening paragraph
- the way he builds tension
- the quotations he includes.

The headline sets up the mystery and asks a question the article might be expected to answer.

The opening paragraph sets out the situation but ends mysteriously, not saying what has happened to the cats.

The writer builds tension by using phrases like 'baffling riddle', 'no one knows why', 'frayed nerves', 'picked off'.

He includes quotations from 'missing' posters and from the local policeman, to give the story authority.

Language and structure

1   Look again at the opening sentence where the author uses a rhetorical device to hook our interest: he might have begun with the phrase '*A rumour*', but instead he writes '*The rumour*'. What is the effect of using the definite article 'the'?

Using 'the' suggests being in the middle of the story – as if readers might already know what the rumour is. This makes them want to read on to find out what rumour is being referred to.

2   Look at PC King's language. It is quite formal and complex.

It is the lack of tangible evidence of these cats which makes us believe something sinister is going on.

a   Why do you think PC King speaks in this formal way? Think about how his language contrasts with that of the other residents.

He sounds much more formal than the other resident quoted. It makes him sound official. He probably speaks in this way because he is aware of his official responsibilities and the fact that he is being interviewed.

b   If he were just chatting to someone more informally, how do you think the policeman might have expressed the same ideas in a more informal way?

Possible rewrite:

We can't find any trace at all of these cats – and that's what makes us think there's something sinister happening.

3   Recounts tell us about events in a chronological sequence. They link sentences and paragraphs together with connectives to show one event developing out of another. Write down two or three connectives you notice the writer using.

Possible answers:

- *this means*
- *but*
- *whatever the answer*
- *the first to vanish*
- *on 2 November . . . a week later . . . a week ago*

Unit 11 Travel writing
Dramatic travel recount: Sinking Fast

Understanding the text

1   How would you describe the weather conditions Steve Callahan is facing?
Severe storm weather

2   Explain what you think the writer means by 'my heart is a pounding pile driver'.
He can feel it pumping as hard as a piece of industrial machinery.

3   Write down two of the emotions Steve Callahan feels towards the end of the extract.
Possible answers:
- *grief at the loss of his boat*
- *disappointed in himself for failing*
- *fear / realization that he will probably die soon.*

Interpreting the text

4   How does the writer make the yacht seem as if it's alive? Look in particular at the language he uses in the second paragraph.
He refers to the boat as 'her'; comparing its movement to a goat climbing a mountain makes it sound alive, like the goat.

5   Look at paragraph 3 in more detail.
  a   How does Steve Callahan use words to recreate the drama of this experience at sea? Look at:
  - his use of vocabulary
  - ways in which he helps the reader to visualize the scene.

  Possible answers:
  Dramatic vocabulary:
  - *he describes the impact as a 'deafening explosion'*
  - *the water 'thunders over me'*
  - *the boat's dive is 'sickening'*
  - *he is surrounded by 'terminal darkness and chaos'*
  - *he describes his final upward escape with the verbs 'rocket' and 'catapult'.*

  Helping the reader visualize the scene:
  - *the water pouring over him is described as if he has been 'thrown into the path of a rampaging river'*
  - *the verbs used to describe him coming out of the boat ('catapult' and 'rocket') make him sound like a firework or something thrown out of machinery, and stress his speed.*

  b   Look at the way he uses sentences to create impact. What do you notice about:
  - his use of very short and much longer sentences? Why does he do this?
  - his mix of statements and questions? What effect does this have?

  Write a short paragraph about this.
  He uses very short sentences to create tension and drama – especially in the third and fourth paragraphs, which convey very dramatic events. Most of the longer sentences in these paragraphs are made up of short phrases and clauses, giving a similar rhythm but in longer, more detailed sentences. He mixes questions and statements in a way that increases the drama and captures the reader's attention.

6   **a**   Look at this sentence:
Unmoving and unconcerned, the moon looks down upon us.

How is the writer presenting the moon here?

As a person; an uninvolved, detached observer

b The writer also uses other rhetorical devices, such as metaphors. Find an example of a metaphor that you think is particularly effective.

Possible answers:

- *'A deafening explosion blankets the subtler sounds' – suggests that this louder sound muffles the quieter ones, like a blanket thrown over something*
- *'Water thunders over me' – conveys the loud thunder-like sound of the water*
- *'The bow points towards its grave' – the sea is referred to as the boat's grave, making the boat sound human*
- *'in the middle of a bucking circus ride' – compares the boat's movement to a circus ride on a bucking bull, giving a visual impression of the amount of movement.*

7 What picture do you get of Steve Callahan from the extract? Does he seem:

calm   disappointed   angry   aggressive   shocked   uncontrolled

Choose the word that you think best fits him, and then write a sentence or two explaining why you have chosen it.

Calm: the pace in the second paragraph does not sound calm, but Callahan seems quite calm at the end of the extract.

Disappointed: he is clearly disappointed at the end of the extract, as he mentions this emotion among others in the last paragraph.

Angry: the way he screams at the canister that will not open suggests anger, but this is not an over-riding emotion in the piece.

Aggressive: no evidence for this.

Shocked: he is not expecting the disaster, so he could be shocked.

Uncontrolled: no evidence for this.

Language and structure

1 Writers use various devices to make their accounts dramatic. Look at this writer's use of punctuation in paragraph 3. Notice how he uses:

- capital letters
- exclamation marks
- dashes.

How do all of these increase the sense of drama?

Capital letters make the word BANG stand out and suggest how loud the noise was.

The exclamation marks suggest excitement, loud noises and sudden action.

The dash to separate ideas in one sentence gives an impression of panicked, scattered thought.

2 The writer uses some very short sentences: 'My soul screams.' 'I yank.' These are used alongside some much longer sentences. What effect would it create if he used:

a abrupt, short sentences all the time?

Personal opinion. It could become monotonous and hard to read.

b longer, more complex sentences all the time?

Personal opinion. It could become less varied and exciting, probably making the action sound less dramatic.

3 The writer uses vivid language to show us the thoughts going through his mind. Look at the way he uses active verbs to increase the drama:

- *my mind **barks** orders*
- *the heavy work **wrings** the air from my lungs*
- *my mind **battles** with my limbs*
- *I **rocket** upward.*

a For each of these, think of a different verb the writer might have used (e.g. 'move' instead of 'rocket').
Possible answers:

- *barks – shouts*
- *wrings – forces*
- *battles – fights*
- *rocket – shoot*

b Describe the different effect of the new word (e.g. 'move' does not have the same sense of speed or rapid movement as 'rocket').
None of the new words has the same force as the originals:

- *'shouts' sounds less urgent than 'barks'*
- *'forces' sounds less physical than 'wrings'*
- *'fights' sounds less strenuous than 'battles'*
- *'shoot' sounds less fast and violent than 'rocket'*

4 Steve Callahan writes a dramatic and often emotional account of being caught in a storm. What would a more factual, less emotional version sound like? Take the main events in the text and write them down in a three-paragraph report, using this frame:

1 Say what we know about the yachtsman.

2 Describe the weather.

3 Describe what happens.

Possible answer:

The yachtsman Steve Callahan was attempting a single-handed journey in his yacht Solo. He was tired out. The weather was very stormy. High seas and strong winds were tossing the boat around.

A sudden crash told Steve that something was badly wrong and the boat was damaged. He had to work quickly to try to get the emergency package out of the hold, and then to get out himself. He succeeded in getting out of the boat but dropped the package. He managed to free the life raft and escape into it as the boat sank.

Descriptive travel recounts: A Desert Dies

Understanding the text

1 What surprises the writer about the storm?
How quickly the wadi fills with water

2 What is the writer most anxious to save from the flood?
His camera and film

3 How has the storm affected some of the camels?
They have become stuck in the mud because they could not move.

4   Name two other effects the storm has.
Possible answers:

- *the thorn trees were all dripping wet*
- *mud was plastered over the tree trunks*
- *many bushes had been uprooted*
- *many of the travellers' belongings were washed away*
- *the writer's camera was full of water*
- *the writer's maps and tobacco were ruined*
- *the travellers' flour and seasoning were soaked and ruined*
- *the saddles and other equipment were waterlogged.*

Interpreting the text

5   Look more closely at the first paragraph. How can you tell that the writer really feels afraid of the storm? Pick out the sentence which you think best shows this.
Personal opinion. Most students will probably pick this sentence:
The water was pouring into the wash from all sides, and for a moment I wondered if we might drown.

6   What impression do you get of the writer from the text? Write a short paragraph about your response to him. Choose some of the words below if you feel they are appropriate. In your paragraph, aim to support each point with an example.
Personal opinion. Possible answers:
afraid, nervous, determined, dismayed, worried, compassionate, patient. (It would be hard to justify the others.)
Good answers will back up each choice of word with evidence from the text, and try to state at which point in the text this characteristic is shown, or whether it runs through the text.

7   What picture do you normally have of the landscape of a desert? In what ways does the picture presented in this text differ from that?
Most people's impression of the desert is of endless yellow-orange sand hills, smoothly undulating over vast distances.
This text informs us that:

- *there are channels for the rain in the desert*
- *there can be violent rain storms*
- *there is grass*
- *there are bushes and thorn trees*
- *the ground can be grey dust, rather than yellow sand.*

8 **a**   What impression do you get of Michael Asher's relationship with the tribes-people? How does he get on with them?
He seems to get on with them quite well: they can share jokes (they laugh together when trying to drag out the camels) and he is clearly taken with their active sense of humour.
He works together with them, and doesn't seem to think he is better than them: they all hunt for their lost possessions together, and they drag out the camels together.
He seems impressed that Wad Fadul managed to find his pipe when he had given up looking for it himself.

b   What impression do you get of his attitude to the camels?
He is fairly indifferent to them, though he seems impressed by their calm resignation as they wait in the mud to be dragged out.

Language and structure

1 One way writers can make descriptions vivid is by using dramatic language. Look at Michael Asher's description of the storm:

I was woken by a clap of thunder that **shook** *the air like an explosion. Streaks of lightning* **forked** *down to the earth, and a second later rain came* **surging** *out of the night sky,* **spattering** *across the dust in enormous droplets.*

Look at the four highlighted verbs. For each one, look at the different word listed below, that the writer might have used:

shook – sounded in

forked – came

surging – falling

spattering – dropping

a Compare the two sets of verbs. Why does Michael Asher's choice of verbs make the storm seem so much more dramatic?

They are highly dramatic verbs, making the storm seem much more active. The replacements are commonplace verbs which can be used in many ways, so they have much less impact.

b Michael Asher also uses a simile:

A clap of thunder that shook the air **like an explosion**

What impression of the thunder does the noun 'explosion' create?

It makes it clear how loud the thunder is, and how sudden. It also makes it sound very threatening, as if there is some intention behind it.

2 Travel writers sometimes use words from the culture they are visiting. Michael Asher uses Arabic words throughout his writing. In this extract he uses the word *wadi*, meaning 'dry river bed'. Some writers might have used the English phrase instead. Why do you think he chooses to use the Arabic term?

Possible answers:

- *because it has a very specific meaning in desert countries, and means something different from what we would imagine when we think of a dry river bed*
- *because he wants to give a strong impression of the culture of where he is travelling*
- *using the local words for things helps to reinforce this sense of a foreign land and culture.*

3 Look at the start of paragraph 2:

The sickly grey light of dawn crept over the world . . .

Some writers might have written: 'Dawn was grey . . .'. What picture of the dawn does the writer's image create?

The light is a very pale grey, and weak. The phrase 'crept over the world' suggests that the light is coming back tentatively after the storm, as if it is afraid.

4 Look at the way the writer describes the scene:

Everywhere the thorn trees glinted and dripped with moisture, and the grey dust had turned into a rippled carpet of ochre mud that was plastered over the tree trunks.

This sentence is rich in description. How might you write it in a less descriptive way, so that it communicated only facts?

Possible rewrite:

Everywhere the thorn trees dripped with water, and the dust had turned to mud which covered the tree trunks.

5 Look at the range of sentences the writer uses in this second paragraph.

- Some of them are chiefly description.
- Some say what happened next.
- Some express an opinion.

Find a sentence that fits each of these functions.

Possible answers:

What happened next:

- *The sickly grey light . . .*
- *I watched my companions . . .*
- *Wad az Zayadi announced that . . .*

Expressing opinion:

- *It was an irony that . . .*
- *None of us was in any mood . . .*

Description:

most of the other sentences in this paragraph

Unit 12 Information texts to persuade
Informing and persuading: Choosing to Be Vegetarian

Understanding the texts

Text A: Leaflet

1 Write down three facts that are included in the text.

Possible answers from the first part (there are others in the rest of the text):

- *almost 7 million people in the UK are now vegetarian or eat meat only once or twice a week*
- *an estimated 5,000 people become vegetarian every week*
- *a vegetarian diet can provide all the necessary nutrients and energy*
- *a healthy vegetarian diet includes plenty of fruit and vegetables, starchy foods, dairy products and alternatives to meat*
- *a vegetarian does not eat fish, meat or poultry and avoids animal by-products*
- *lacto-ovo vegetarians make up the majority of vegetarians*
- *lacto-ovo vegetarians eat dairy products and eggs*
- *lacto-vegetarians don't eat eggs*
- *vegans consume no animal products at all*
- *demi-vegetarians are relatively new*
- *demi-vegetarians don't eat red meat, but occasionally eat white meat or fish.*

2 Look at the first sentence. Are the 7 million people mentioned all vegetarians?

No, some of them still eat meat once or twice a week.

3 What three reasons are given for people choosing a vegetarian lifestyle?

Reasons:

- *an interest in food and health*
- *concerns over animal welfare*
- *concerns about the environment.*

4 The leaflet gives information about different types of vegetarians. Which is the newest category?

Demi-vegetarians

5 How many Sainsbury's products carry the 'Healthy Balance' symbol?
Around 2,000

Text B: Website

6 Write down three facts that are included in the text.
Possible answers from the first section (there are others in the rest of the text):
- *in the UK, 800 million animals are killed for food each year*
- *these animals are just as feeling as household pets*
- *many of these animals are far more intelligent than household pets*
- *they are denied access to their young*
- *they are fed on unnatural diets and chemicals*
- *they are kept in cramped conditions*
- *they often develop physical and psychological problems*
- *they are transported around a lot*
- *some of them are taken to markets abroad*
- *this is a long and stressful journey.*

7 What reasons does this text suggest for being a vegetarian?
Any of these reasons:
- *to reduce animal suffering and slaughter*
- *to reduce the ways animal farming is harming the planet (contributing to the greenhouse effect, acid rain, destruction of the rain forests, over-fishing, extinction of species, soil erosion)*
- *to make more efficient use of natural resources*
- *to contribute positively to the planet's future.*

8 How does meat production damage rain forests?
People destroy millions of hectares of rain forest a year to create land for grazing animals.

Interpreting the texts

9 Look at the three images in text A. What are they supposed to show the reader? Describe what each image shows. Then write a sentence saying why you think it has been chosen and how it helps persuade readers to think about becoming vegetarian.

Describe the image	Explain why you think it has been chosen
Young woman eating a supposedly vegetarian sandwich and smiling	The sandwich looks nice: this and her smile suggest that being a vegetarian isn't dull and doesn't mean you won't enjoy your food. She also looks healthy, suggesting that a vegetarian diet is good for you.
Bread and a range of vegetables	The food looks fresh and shows a range of colours, suggesting that vegetarian food is healthy because it is fresh, and that it is bright, varied and interesting.
Young executive types at a table with vegetarian meals in front of them. They are smiling and talking.	The people look young, healthy and successful, and are clearly enjoying themselves. The image suggests that if you eat vegetarian food you might be more like these people.

10 Look at the image in text B. Write a sentence about why it has been selected. How would this image help persuade a reader to think about becoming a vegetarian?

Any of these points could be made:

- *the pig is in an enclosed space, suggesting that it is imprisoned, and that it wants to get out*
- *the pig is looking straight at the camera, as though it is appealing to your better nature to help it*
- *the pig looks cute and defenceless.*

11 Look at text A. Is the text purely an information leaflet, or is it also an advertisement for Sainsbury's? How can you tell?

It is really an advert for Sainsbury's vegetarian food. Although it contains general information, it is largely about their food labelling and how it helps vegetarians and other people wanting to eat a healthy diet.

12 Who do you think the two texts may be aimed at?

a vegetarians

b people thinking of becoming vegetarians

c meat eaters

d people interested in food and health

e older people

f younger people

Choose the *two* groups from the list above that you think are most suitable for each text, and write a sentence explaining why.

Text A possible answers:

a – because it offers advice on the range of foods available to them from the shop, and on healthy eating for them

b – because it encourages them by describing the range of foods available and how they can eat a balanced diet; contains aspirational images

c – unlikely, although its information on what a vegetarian is might be helpful if they have vegetarian friends

d – because it is largely about a balanced diet

e – unlikely, because it is designed in a 'young' way

f – because the design and style of text is quite friendly and informal

Text B possible answers:

a – because it assumes that vegetarianism solves all the problems highlighted, so vegetarians would be the most sympathetic audience

b – because it is propaganda, working on meat-eating guilt to try to convert them

c – unlikely; it is so negative about meat eating that it would put them off reading it

d – unlikely, as it doesn't talk about health issues

e – not clear: could be, as it is written in a formal way

f – not clear: its style does not suggest a particular aim at young people; some students may argue that young people are more likely to be vegetarian than older ones and so they constitute the main audience for the text

Language and structure

1 In information texts we often expect statements. Persuasive texts usually use more commands, where the verb is at the start ('*Eat* some of these foods each day').

In text A find:

a one statement

Any sentence from page one and the first column of page two and:

- *Fresh, frozen, canned, dried and juiced varieties all count.*
- *Fruit and vegetables provide many vitamins and minerals . . .*
- *The general healthy eating advice given to the general population also applies to vegetarians.*
- *A healthy diet includes plenty of fruit and vegetables . . .*

b one command.

Any of these:

- *Aim to eat at least five portions of fruit and vegetables a day.*
- *Eat some of these foods everyday . . .*
- *Eat a variety of these foods to ensure . . .*

2 We expect information texts to use factual language. This might include technical terms. Look at these technical terms and re-read the passage in text A where they are used. Write down what you think the highlighted part of each word might mean:

a **lacto**-vegetarians

milk-consuming

b lacto-**ovo** vegetarians

egg-eating

c **demi**-vegetarians

half

3 Persuasive texts often use **emotive** words. These are words intended to get an emotional response from readers. Examples in text B are:

They're transported . . . to the horrors of the slaughterhouse

Dolphins and whales are indiscriminately killed

a Think of some more neutral words which could have been used in these two examples.

Possible answers:

They are taken to the abattoir

Dolphins and whales are accidentally caught

b What is the effect of replacing the emotive words with more neutral ones?

The sentences become less forceful and persuasive.

4 In narrative texts, the paragraphs usually have to go in a certain order to make sense. In persuasive information texts, there is a less obvious story to tell. Look at the organization of the first six paragraphs in text B.

a For each of paragraphs 2–6 write down the word or phrase which is used to link it to the paragraph before. You should look for examples of:

Pronouns: *it / they / these / them*

Connectives: *despite this / then / yet / even / next / so*

Paragraph 2: these

Paragraph 3: yet, they

Paragraph 4: then, they

Paragraph 5: some

Paragraph 6: they, then

b Would it be possible for these paragraphs to be organized in a different order? Could the text still make sense? Explain why or why not.

No, because they are organized to tell a story to some extent, and the information in each paragraph builds on the ones before.

Unit 13 Explanations
Explaining a scientific report: Tollund Man

Understanding the text

1 How did scientists work out that the man must have been put in the bog around 2,000 years earlier?

Because he was buried just above a layer of moss which they knew was formed in the early Iron Age, about 2,000 years ago

2 How old was he?

Not old, but over 20

3 How could scientists tell his age?

He must have been over 20 because his wisdom teeth had grown.

4 What is known about the way he died?

He probably died as a result of the noose tied around his neck.

5 What clue was there that a special occasion had taken place?

His last meal had been made up of things which had to be collected very carefully and possibly saved, as they could be hard to find.

Interpreting the text

6 What can you deduce from the man's last meal about the community he lived in and their habits?

The cultivated seeds suggest that these people farmed. There was no meat in his stomach so they might have been vegetarian or only eaten meat rarely. Some of the seeds were gathered, so the community didn't rely entirely on farming for its food.

7 What mysteries are there surrounding the death of Tollund Man?

Who he was and why he was killed

8 The text contains many factual details.

  a Write down one fact.

  Any sentence apart from the three questions in paragraph 3

  b Does it contain any personal opinions? If so, write them down; if not, explain why not.

  No – because it is a purely factual account of what happened and the result of scientific investigations

Language and structure

1 Like most explanatory texts, this one is written in the third-person form. It never uses the pronouns 'I' or 'me'.

  a Why do you think this is?

  Because it is a factual report and not meant to be personal

  b Would the worksheet be less or more interesting to read if it used a more personal style?

  Personal opinion. Good answers will back up their opinion with a reason.

2 Look at the first sentence under the heading 'Scientific report on the body'. It uses the passive voice ('The body was removed . . . by . . .').

  a How could the writer have written this sentence using the active voice?

  Doctors and scientists removed the body and examined it.

  b Why do you think the passive voice has been used?

Because it is not important who removed the body, only who examined it. The sentence does not really say who removed it.

3 The worksheet is aimed at students aged about 14. What clues are there in the language that this is the writer's target audience, rather than doctors and scientists?

You might comment on:

- the length and types of sentences
- the structure of the explanation
- the use of vocabulary.

The sentences are all quite short and relatively simple, with very little use of the passive; easy to understand. The explanation is clearly structured into sections: how the body was found, and then the three areas investigated by the scientists – very clear and easy to follow. The questions at the end of the first section encourage the audience to read on and find out more.

The vocabulary is not particularly complicated – it is easy to understand without using a dictionary.

4 Look at the structure of the worksheet:

- general introduction
- three subheadings with explanations beneath each one.

Could the subheadings ('Date of burial, Cause of death, His last meal') have been placed in any order, or did it need to be this particular order?

There could be another order, although this order suggests the order in which things were examined: dating the site, then examining the man closely and using X-rays to find out more physical details about him, and finally cutting him open to find out about his last meal. This order also moves from the general (site and age, etc.) to very specific details.

5 Choose two sentences whose meaning is linked, and show how the writer links the ideas in the second sentence back to the ideas in the first. What are the linking words or phrases?

Possible answers (there are others in the text):

- *Two men were cutting peat for the tile stove and the kitchen range. **As they** worked . . .*
- *The man lay on his right side just as if he was asleep. **He** lay . . .*
- *The air of gentle peace . . . was shattered when a small lump of peat was removed from beside his head. **Underneath** was a rope . . . twisted together. **This** was a noose.*
- *He was not an old man . . . his wisdom teeth had grown. He had **therefore** probably . . .*
- *There were no traces . . . had lived for 12–24 hours after this meal. **In other words** he had not . . .*

Unit 14 Playing with non-fiction conventions
Parody of a newspaper report: The Glamis Herald

Understanding the text

1 Write down two features which make the text look like a real newspaper.

Any two of the following:

- *banner across the top*
- *headline*
- *subheadings*
- *type styles*
- *photo*
- *set out in columns*

87

- *'On other pages' section.*

2 What is the gist of the 'story' that the text is reporting?

That Macbeth is defending his wife against allegations that she may have had something to do with the death of Duncan

3 Who is Banquo, according to the article?

A long-term associate of Macbeth, and possibly a banker

4 Why is Hillary Macbeth upset?

Because of the allegations about the deaths of Duncan and Banquo

Interpreting the text

5 The text makes a lot of jokey references to *Macbeth*. Imagine the newspaper is being read by someone who does not know Shakespeare's play. Choose one of the examples below and explain the joke:

   a The recent 'Duncangate' allegations

     In the play, Lady Macbeth plots the murder of Duncan, king of Scotland, and Macbeth carries it out. The suffix '-gate' alludes to the 'Watergate' scandal in the US.

   b Weather Forecast for Tomorrow and Tomorrow and Tomorrow

     Macbeth has a famous speech which starts 'Tomorrow and tomorrow and tomorrow . . .'

   c Cooking Tips with the Weird Sisters

     The weird sisters are the three witches Macbeth meets at the beginning of the play; they are seen placing unpleasant ingredients into a cauldron.

6 The text also makes reference to ex-President Clinton and his wife. What does the author's style suggest about his attitude towards them?

The way he compares them to the Macbeths suggests that he does not think they can be trusted.

7 These are some of the features we expect in newspapers. For each one, write down an example from this text.

Feature	Example
Headline to grab the reader's attention	*Macbeth defends wife – 'Saintly, selfless public servant' says former Thane*
Byline (telling us the name of the writer)	*by Henry The Porter*
Subheadings to break up the text	*Cawdor What A Scorcher*
A topic sentence which tells the whole story at the start of the article	*The controversial new king of Scotland, King Macbeth, today spoke out in defence of his wife, Lady Hillary Macbeth, whom many critics have called 'the power behind the throne'.*
Trails for other features in the newspaper	*On Other Pages*
Advertising	*Out Damned Spot . . .* *Hands sweetened! . . .*

8 Write a short paragraph about your response to the text.

   a What do you like about it? Which jokes do you find funny? Which bits do not make sense? How could it be funnier?

Personal opinion. Students should try to answer all parts of the question.

b   What does it suggest to you about the writer's attitude to powerful politicians, and the way they are usually presented in newspaper reports?

It suggests that reports tend to focus on people's reactions and the public relations side of things, rather than the actual facts; that politicians 'get away with murder'.

Language and structure

1   Newspaper headlines often have certain key features. Look at the features below and write down an example from this text.

a   They use the present tense.

Macbeth defends wife – 'Saintly, selfless public servant' says former Thane

b   They use alliteration (repetition of initial consonants).

Saintly, selfless, servant, says

c   They are telegrammatic – they miss out grammatical words like *the / his / their*.

'Macbeth defends wife' not 'Macbeth defends his wife'

2   The sentence style in newspapers often uses a lot of modification. This means giving as much detail as possible in each sentence. Take this sentence:

An English teacher today bought a new car.

Reported in a newspaper, this might begin:

Trendy English teacher Jez Foley, 24, yesterday amazed pupils at Long Melford High School . . .

Notice how the writer uses labels ('trendy', '24') to add details to the subject of the sentence.

Now look at the first sentence of the *Glamis Herald*. How does the writer use a similar technique in writing about Macbeth?

The article doesn't just say 'King Macbeth', but 'the controversial new king of Scotland, King Macbeth'.

3   Newspapers sometimes use the passive voice, like this:

Suggestions that the king may have 'seen ghosts' were dismissed by an official spokesman.

a   Write this sentence in the active voice.

An official spokesman dismissed suggestions that the king may have 'seen ghosts'.

b   Why do you think newspapers sometimes use the passive voice in this way?

It highlights the suggestions, rather than the person dismissing (or making) them.

4   Some of the writing in the text is funny because of its reference to *Macbeth* or the Clintons. Some is funny because it uses wordplay or puns.

Choose one example from those below and explain how the writer is playing with words:

a   Cawdor What a Scorcher

Play on typical newspaper headline 'Cor! What a scorcher' in hot weather. Cawdor is another of Macbeth's titles.

b   Angus McDeayton

Angus Deayton is a comedy personality who does a lot of advertising. To connect the advert to the Macbeth story and the 'Scottish' newspaper, the writer has made him sound more Scottish, by adding 'Mc' to the front of his name.

c   Ian Macbethkill.

Ian McAskill is a weather presenter. He already has a Scottish-sounding name, so the writer has connected him to the Macbeth story by changing his name to include 'Macbeth'.

Unit 1 PCM A

Healthy eating

Tips to make a formal leaflet:

- keep pictures to a minimum and ensure they are more formal
- stick to a uniform style of layout, e.g. use one style of bullet points and don't combine text and distracting illustrations
- use an impersonal tone and avoid 'you', e.g. 'Evidence shows that people consume 100 tonnes of food in a lifetime'
- avoid informal headings such as 'Fun Facts'
- don't shorten words, e.g. use 'carbohydrates' not 'carbs'; use 'vegetables' not 'veggies'
- if using ICT avoid fun fonts.

Here are some prompts to get you started.

Foods can be classified into the following four main categories:

A balanced diet can be achieved by . . .

Broader food categories are macronutrients and micronutrients.

Macronutrients are . . .

Micronutrients are . . .

Experts in nutrition advise that an average person should consume . . .

Unit 2 PCM A

My first day at school

What do each of these people remember about their first day at school? List two or three main points for each person.

Name	Best known as	Main points
Esther Rantzen		• • •
Glenys Kinnock		• • •
Brian Keenan		• • •
Benjamin Zephaniah		• • •

Unit 2 PCM B

My first day at school

Use some of these ideas to help you write your recount.

Beginning

As I approached the school gates . . .

Walking to school for the first time I noticed . . .

Before reaching school I . . .

I watched my mum/dad depart for the first time and I . . .

The school buildings were . . .

The bell rang as . . .

Initially I thought that . . .

To start with it seemed . . .

My initial impression was . . .

Middle

I looked around the classroom and noticed . . .

The classroom was full of fun things to do and . . .

My teacher was called . . . and he/she looked . . .

I was relieved when I was finally introduced to my teacher because . . .

In contrast to being at home, school was . . .

Next I . . .

After that we . . .

Meanwhile . . .

Also . . .

Then . . .

End

Finally, the day came to an end and I . . .

Eventually the school bell rang to mark the end of my first day at school and I . . .

After all . . .

Consequently I . . .

As a result of my first day at school I was . . .

When my mum/dad collected me I . . .

Looking back it now seems . . .

I can't believe that I . . .

In conclusion, my first day at school was . . .

Unit 3 PCM A
Similarities and differences

These pointers may help you get started:

What advice do the texts offer?

Do both texts state that mobile phones carry a health risk?

What is the layout and design?

How do the texts begin?

Are they aimed at the same audience?

Are they personal or impersonal?

What person are they written in?

I noticed that the information in the two texts was similar in the following ways:

-
-
-
-
-
-

I noticed that the information in the two texts was different in the following ways:

-
-
-
-
-
-

Unit 5 PCM A
Planning a description

Look at the examples below. Then add further examples of your own.

Adjectives

As I walked along the *tranquil* beach the *refreshing* water lapped against my *warm* toes.

-
-

Adverbs

I *lazily* sauntered back to my hotel room.

-
-

Similes

The sun glistened like a new gold coin.

-
-

Metaphors

The atmosphere in the evening was electric.

-
-

Senses

I could *hear* the children frolicking in the pool.

The *smell* of bacon frying greeted me as I entered the restaurant for breakfast.

-
-

Feelings

A *feeling* of total relaxation hit me as I walked off the plane.

-
-

Unit 6 PCM A

Writing a formal newspaper report: 1

Headline:

Paragraph 1: *mention the plane, the pilot and where the event happened.*

Residents of Canterbury were last night reported to be furious after . . .

Paragraph 2: *try to use a sympathetic tone for the statement. Think of abstract nouns you could use.*

This morning stranded pilot, Glyn Hughes, sent a statement of apology to the people of Canterbury. In it he says, "The whole event is one that I would like to forget. I . . .

Paragraph 3: *bring out the residents' fears and the possible danger they were in.*

Local councillor, Leigh Fisher, told reporters, "I was shocked to hear . . .

Paragraph 4: *emphasize the seriousness of the event using words like 'irresponsible' 'grave' and 'hazardous'.*

Police officers have launched an official enquiry, insisting the owners of Biggin Hill Flying Club explain . . .

Paragraph 5: *refer to a similar event that ended tragically, for emphasis.*

Some of the older residents remember the fateful event of April 1974, where . . .

Unit 6 PCM B

Writing a formal newspaper report: 2

Paragraph 1:

Summarize the events at Canterbury Airfield in one paragraph. Briefly make reference to the who?, what?, where?, when? and why? Do not expand on any point. The detail will come later in the report.

Paragraph 2:

Focus on the what? and expand slightly on the when? Make reference to the plane, accident with the brakes, and the pilot's sequence of actions that led to the incident.

Paragraph 3:

Focus on the who? Expand your article by giving details about the pilot, Glynn Hughes. Refer not only to his age but also to his profession and series of oversights that morning.

Paragraph 4:

Focus on the where? Bring the reader's attention to the area where the incident took place and describe it in detail. Make reference to the position of the airfield, the nearby forest, residents' houses and the motorway.

Points to remember:

Include formal connectives such as It is reported that . . ., Allegedly . . ., Evidence proves that . . . to structure your article.

Do not offer your own opinion and try to leave out sensationalist vocabulary.

Unit 7 PCM A

Autobiographical writing

Event:

Paragraph 1:

Possible connectives: to start with, it all began, firstly, in the beginning

Paragraphs 2, 3 and 4:

Possible connectives: next, as well as, also, secondly/thirdly, so, in fact, then

Paragraph 5:

Possible connectives: finally, at the end, eventually, above all, for all that, therefore.

Unit 8 PCM A

Florence Nightingale

Heading: *think of an attention-grabbing heading that will entice your readers to find out more, e.g. 'The Amazing Lady with the Lamp'.*

Significant dates:

-
-
-
-

Significant achievements / awards:

-
-
-
-

Career details:

-
-
-

Interesting historical facts:

-
-
-

Other interesting points:

-
-
-

Will you use:

- third person yes / no
- statements yes / no
- past or present tense (circle one or both)
- questions? yes / no

Unit 9 PCM A

Writing survey: writing for different subjects

The subject that requires the most writing from me is . . .

because . . .

The subject that requires the least writing from me is . . .

because . . .

The subject that requires the most formal style is . . .

because . . .

The subject that encourages the most detail in my writing is . . .

because . . .

The subject that requires the least description is . . .

because . . .

Unit 9 PCM B

Writing an explanation

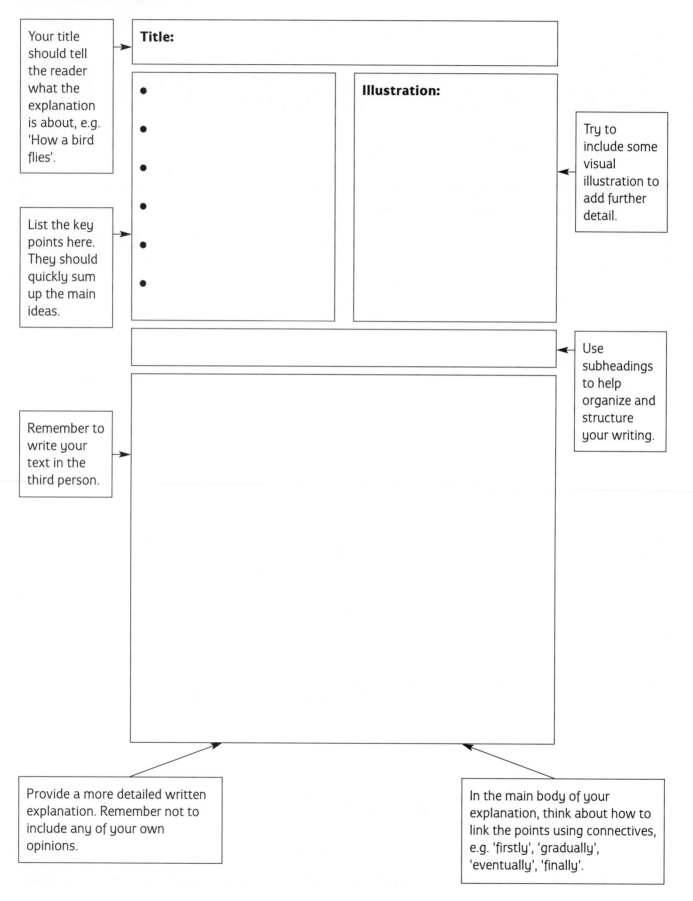

Your title should tell the reader what the explanation is about, e.g. 'How a bird flies'.

Title:

Illustration:

Try to include some visual illustration to add further detail.

List the key points here. They should quickly sum up the main ideas.

Use subheadings to help organize and structure your writing.

Remember to write your text in the third person.

Provide a more detailed written explanation. Remember not to include any of your own opinions.

In the main body of your explanation, think about how to link the points using connectives, e.g. 'firstly', 'gradually', 'eventually', 'finally'.

Unit 10 PCM A
Writing an informal newspaper report

THE TAWTON EXPRESS

Police have no clue!

Date:

Yesterday, a gunshot was overheard . . .

Photo:

Police chief 'embarrassed'

PC Evans, who was first on the scene, commented, '. . .

Professor Plum found the funny side of the incident later, claiming, '. . .

Miss Scarlet reacted angrily to her arrest, vowing, 'I will . . .

Local resident Charlie Braham laughed as he told our reporter, 'Bagshot Manor is always . . .

After the mistake had been explained , . . .

Finally, PC Evans made a promise to . . .

Reporter:
(student's name)

Unit 11 PCM A

Describing a journey

Opening line: use an active verb to describe how you shut the door behind you.

e.g. *The door splintered as I forced it into the frame.*

Describe the road outside your house, using the third person.

e.g. *The road was grimy, just like everywhere in this town.*

Describe the length of your journey using a simile or metaphor.

e.g. *Leila's house was only five minutes away, but seemed more like a trek across an urban desert.*

Add some interest to your plot, such as an unexpected feature on your journey.

e.g. *Suddenly, the dull quiet was smashed as . . .*

Use a short, abrupt sentence to continue the drama.

e.g. *Time to run.*

Include opinion; what details in your surroundings bring out an emotion (e.g. hatred, fear, surprise or affection)?

e.g. *The splinters of glass scattered across the tarmac hurried me along.*

To end your description, convey an emotion by describing a reaction of the senses.

e.g. *My mouth tasted of blood as adrenalin rushed me into the safety of the porch.*

Unit 12 PCM A

Writing a leaflet

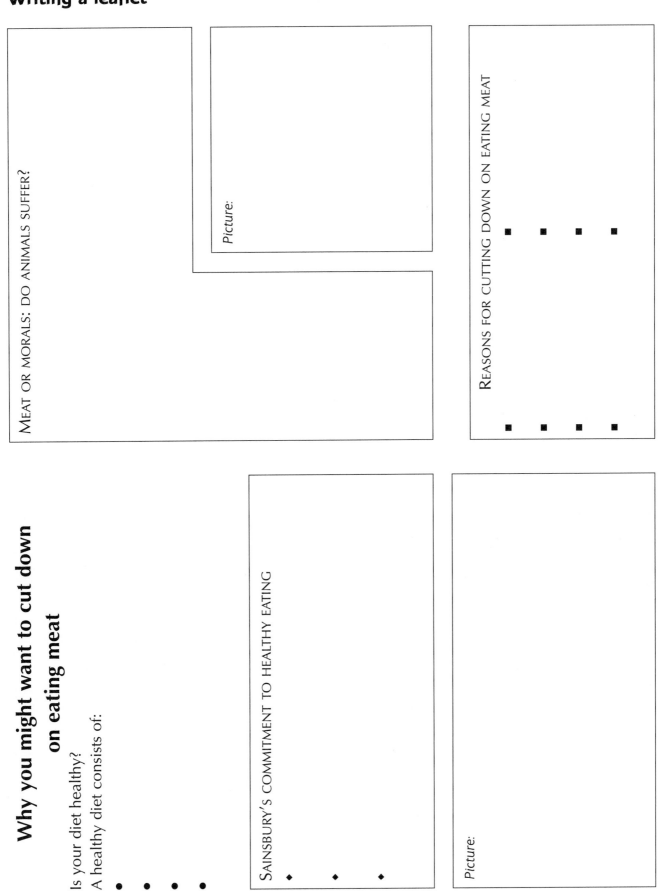

MEAT OR MORALS: DO ANIMALS SUFFER?

Picture:

REASONS FOR CUTTING DOWN ON EATING MEAT

Why you might want to cut down on eating meat

Is your diet healthy?
A healthy diet consists of:

SAINSBURY'S COMMITMENT TO HEALTHY EATING

Picture:

Unit 13 PCM A
Tollund Man History assignment

Write one sentence in each box to form a complete paragraph.

> Who was Tollund Man?

> What did the people who discovered him originally think they had found?

> Describe his physical state when discovered.

> Mention one detail about why he will be useful to scientists.

> End the paragraph with how he might have been killed.

Unit 13 PCM B
Tollund Man English assignment

Write one sentence in each box to form a complete paragraph.

Opening line: use an active verb to describe the sounds as you are dug up.

Describe your reaction to coming into the light again, using the first person.

Describe the faces of the scientists using a simile or metaphor. Do you want them to seem like saviours, or more threatening?

Use a short, abrupt sentence to continue the drama.

End the paragraph with a statement of your opinion; convey an emotion by describing a reaction of the senses.

Unit 14 PCM A

Writing a parody: estate agent's report

Dunsinane Castle

The imposing features of Dunsinane Castle make this a tempting purchase for any budding Scottish Lord! Built in the 12th century, this four-storey stone building has been the scene for some of history's greatest battles, not least the defeat of King Macbeth by the enraged son of the murdered King Duncan.

Birnam Wood still flourishes at the bottom of the hill, but potential buyers should beware any movement towards the castle! The beautiful surrounding moorlands make Dunsinane Castle a real steal at just £1,000,000.

Conventions of an estate agent report:

- impersonal voice

- often informal and exaggerated style, e.g. 'any budding Scottish Lord!'

- information text, e.g. 'Built in the 12th century'

- persuasive language, e.g. 'tempting', 'greatest', 'beautiful'

Write your estate agent report here.

General PCM 1
Brainstorming

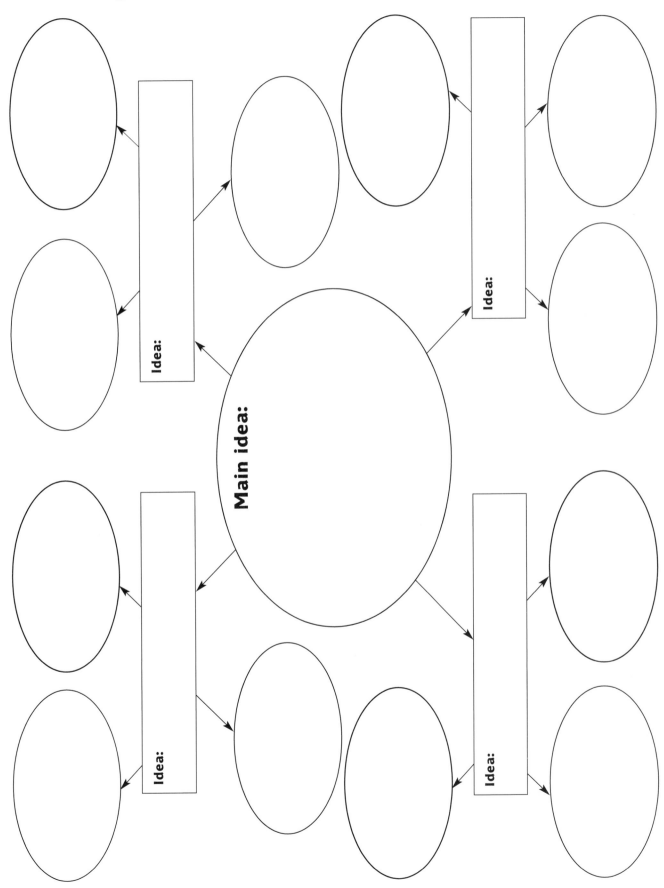

General PCM 2

Brainstorming for arguments

Point under discussion:

Ideas for

Evidence / examples / quotes

Ideas against

Evidence / examples / quotes

Any conclusions reached:

General PCM 3

Key words

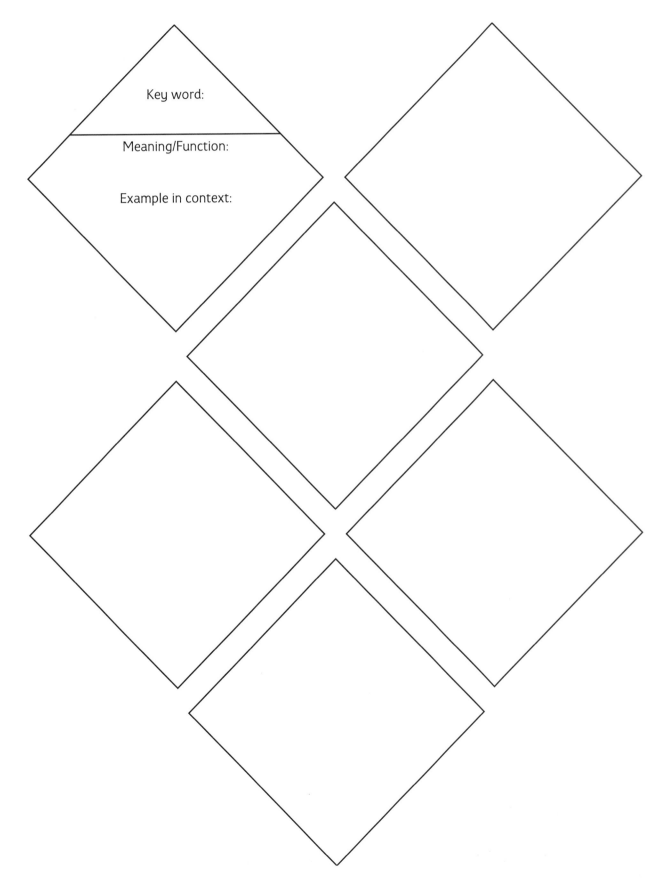

Key word:

Meaning/Function:

Example in context:

General PCM 4
Research grid

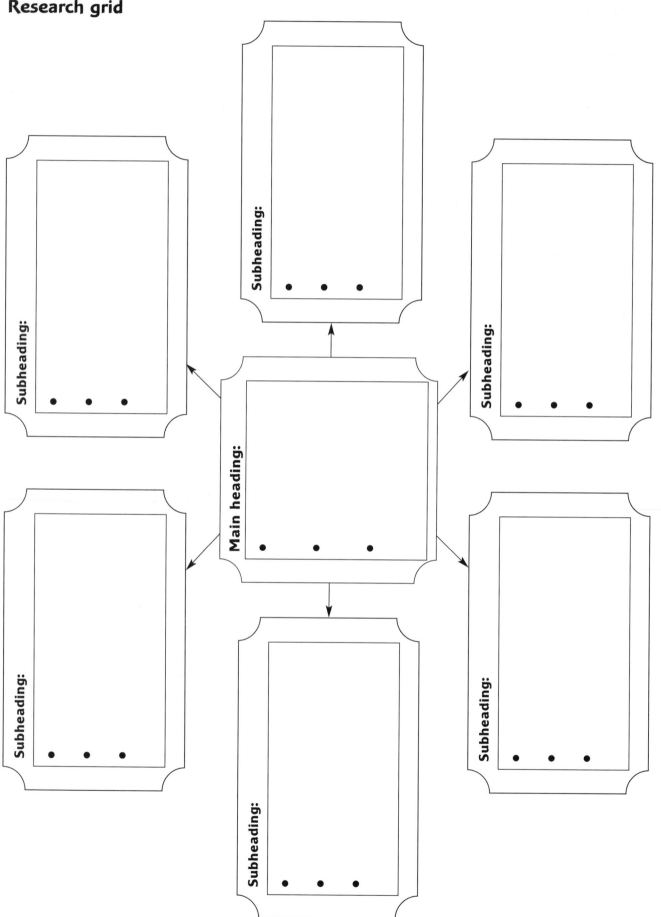

General PCM 5

Information

Information text	Why might you use this particular information text?
A dictionary	To discover the meaning of a word.

General PCM 6
Recount

Detail	Examples
Is it written in first person narrative?	
Does this extract have a variety of sentence structure? (short, simple and complex)	
Is there any use of connectives to add to chronology? E.g. Initially, eventually …	
Is it wriiten in the past tense? If so provide examples.	
Does the writer concentrate on an event that interests the reader? Provide an example.	
Does the writer offer some detail and/or extra comment on the event being referred to?	

Recount text should have the following:

1.

2.

3.

4.

General PCM 7

Explanation

	Yes... now provide examples to show that you understand.	No... put a cross in the box.
Is it written in the present tense?		
Are there any causal connectives?		
Is any specialised terminology used?		
Are there any examples of illustrations/diagrams/flow charts etc? If so, why do you think they are present?		
Does the title indicate what is being written about?		
Can you find any connectives that help to sequence the text?		
Is it written in the third person?		
Is it written in the active voice?		

General PCM 8

Types of writing used in subjects

Research survey: **What forms of writing do I use in this subject?**	
Name of subject: Forms of writing used:	
Which non-fiction text type does this form most lend itself to?	
What person do I write in? (first/second/third)	
Do I use the past or present tense?	
Is the layout of my writing important?	
Do I need to use connectives? If so, which in particular?	
Do I use the passive or active voice?	
Is there a need to organise my writing chronologically?	
Is there a variety of sentence structures of does one type prevail? (E.g. simple and compound sentences)	
Is there a concentration on one type of vocabulary? If so, why? (E.g. descriptive, technical, informal, formal)	
Any other notable features?	

General PCM 9

Conventions of different types of writing

The main conventions of _____ writing are:
1.
2.
3.
4.
5.
6.
7.

The main conventions of _____ writing are:
1.
2.
3.
4.
5.
6.
7.

General PCM 10
Instruction texts

Purpose:

Equipment:

Instructions:

1. First, . . .

2. Take . . .

3. Then . . .

4. Put . . .

5. Next, . . .

6. Don't forget . . .

7. Place . . .

8. Finally . . .

Final tips:

General PCM 11

Speaking and listening

Opening: *state your point of view. Grab the listeners' attention, perhaps with rhetorical questions.*

Develop your point: *give reasons and evidence to prove your point, using statistics and emotive language to persuade.*

Show you understand the opposing view: *state why others may disagree with you, but use a tone which suggests they cannot be believed.*

Counter argument: *explain why you are right, and they are wrong. Back up each point with evidence and a comment.*

Final summary: *summarize your point of view. Include a 'kick-line' at the end to leave listeners thinking, using a final emotive statement or rhetorical question.*